TIM GENT

CANOE CAMPING

Photographs by Tim and Susannah Gent

First published in 2014

Published in Great Britain 2014 by Pesda Press

Tan y Coed Canol

Ceunant

Caernarfon

Gwynedd

LL55 4RN

Copyright © 2014 Tim Gent

ISBN   978-1-906095-48-2

The Author asserts the moral right to be identified as the author of this work.

Printed and bound in Poland, www.hussarbooks.pl

Dedication

While responsible for everything in this book, including any embedded errors, so much that has found its way in has been the result of teamwork. Although canoe camping makes a fine endeavour for the lone participant – at least one who knows what they're doing – my good fortune has been to undertake all my trips in company.

This has provided me with someone to help lug heaps of kit from van to canoe and from canoe to campsite – and then back again; someone to stand patiently holding a paddle, pan or Prospector (sometimes for a very long time) while I work out camera lens apertures or wait for the sun to finally poke its head around a cloud; someone to take extremely good photos of me; and someone to share each wonderful and sometimes not so wonderful outdoor experience that a shared life of camping, canoeing, hillwalking and everything else has had to offer. Need I say more?

Contents

About the Author

Tim has enjoyed an outdoor life since childhood. Farming, forestry conservation and archaeology have provided a working environment in the field, and contributed to an understanding of the land. While paddling and camping from Arctic Scandinavia to the Mediterranean coast, he has absorbed more, and hopes he is still learning.

Writing about fishing, hillwalking, canoeing and camping, Tim had the first of many magazine articles published in 1990. He is a regular contributor to *Canoe and Kayak UK* and *Bushcraft and Survival Skills*, and often writes for *The Great Outdoors*.

When not camping, Tim and Susannah live in Devon, England, midway between Dartmoor and the Atlantic coast.

Introduction

Early morning sunlight crept across the groundsheet, inching another fine day towards us. Not wanting to miss anything during the short summer night, we'd left the entrance flap open, and the alluring blue-grey flicker of nearby waves soon had us up and out.

Half an hour later, refreshed by tea and filled with homemade muesli, we left our tent to become better acquainted with its little wooded island and paddled across the lake to where a wild river thundered over broad rocky shelves. Fresh from the remains of a distant snowfield, the water was a touch cooler than we'd hoped, but a little further along the pine and birch-studded shore we found a shallow flat-bottomed bay. Here, the bed was a smooth expanse of soft, golden sand, the water warmed by two weeks of almost constant sun. Soon the grime of the last few days' travel was gone.

Of course camping isn't always quite this idyllic. Sat almost exactly over Sweden's little segment of the Arctic Circle, this early August attempt at night must rank as one of our most memorable, but few nights spent under canvas disappoint, and with the correct kit, and armed with a few useful tricks and strategies, even the wildest or coldest nocturnal offering can be as snug and enjoyable as any spent at home.

Few canoeists will pass up the opportunity to spend as much of the day as possible under an open sky, pushing their vessel on as far as tired arms will take it, out to somewhere special. This book is designed to assist all those that, having made their way to where they can breathe deep and witness the world, might wish to prolong the experience by spending the night under the stars. Why turn back at the end of the day when you can pull ashore and create a home? Instead, wake in the morning as the flash and shimmer of the sun reflecting off nearby waves calls you on to another day of exploration and fulfilment.

Of course we canoeists are blessed. Not only do we have a vessel that provides the chance to break free and wander, but we possess a craft that has so much more to offer. When the indigenous people of northern America first developed the canoe they needed a workhorse. Living within a heavily wooded landscape in which only rivers and lakes offered easy movement, they required something to carry firewood, building materials, baskets of berries or the results of a successful day's hunting. It had to be lightweight, easily repaired with what was available from the nearby forest, yet still able to transport them to the nearest fishing ground or carry the family and all their belongings from one shore to another. I like to think that with time and experiment they produced something of almost unparalleled beauty and practicality.

What we lucky modern canoeists have inherited then is a vessel that has been fine-tuned by need and circumstance over many generations. We own a simple, clean and silent craft that is still just as beautiful and still just as good at moving us around. Importantly, it also remains just as successful at carrying loads, sometimes heavy loads. These cargoes can include almost anything that might improve or enhance our outdoor experience, particularly if the experience we choose is to camp.

Why turn back at the end of the day when you can pull ashore and create a home?

Camping connects us with a not so distant and very significant past. Even us western Europeans, now unquestionably urbanised, have experienced a sedentary existence for only a fraction of our evolution. For most of human existence we have been mobile, making our temporary home where conditions or resources most appeal. Camping is in our blood. Camping almost anywhere a little wild appeals. Spending time under canvas somewhere out of the way touches at those experiences that have formed and fashioned our very character. It can be profoundly satisfying.

Not surprisingly then, my hope is to encourage anyone with even a touch of the explorer about them to head out onto the water with a tent lying happily at the bottom of their canoe. I recognise though that despite this ambition, and an intention to cover as many aspects of canoe camping as possible, I can't cater for every element of basic boat handling and ownership here. There just isn't the space.

This might be a serious concern with regard to those lacking paddling experience. Fortunately however, training in boatcraft is offered by a range of individuals and organisations. Guidance is also available in print, and I can refer you to *Canoeing* by Ray Goodwin, or Bill Mason's classic *Path of the Paddle*. Those fundamental canoeing skills needed before embarking on a camping trip can be found beyond the this book. I don't need to worry if I can't fit everything in.

In the following chapters I hope to offer enough sound advice to allow anyone who has mastered the use of a canoe to put it all into soul-invigorating practice. In short, I hope this book can offer something to all – a guide to those who are already using their canoe to explore, but keen now to know a little more about taking the next step, and also some practical advice to those future canoeists who, after reading it all, feel the need to find somebody to show them how to push off from the shore for the first time.

For some of course it may never be possible to go canoe camping. For them, I hope that the contents of this book might allow for a little of the enjoyment, even if only in the imagination.

How this book is laid out

Some seasoned tent dwellers may well only want to know how to take all their existing camping gear and knowledge, and unite it with a canoe. Others will be informed and practised canoeists, who just haven't yet had the chance to put up a tent at the end of a day's exploration. For those in either group I hope you can overlook the sections where I deal with matters you already know about.

I have split the book into five main sections:

What to take – covering everything from saucepans to spare paddles, tent pegs to torches.

What to take it all in – canoe choice.

How to take everything – the best ways to pack and protect your kit before it meets its transportation, and then how to fit it all in.

Where to go – addressing the question of both where you are able to go, and how best to choose a good trip from the available areas.

Making the most of the journey – discussing ways to make the trip as enjoyable as possible.

What to do when you get there – looking at everything from selecting a campsite, to packing up when you're finally ready to leave. This section considers essential tasks such as cooking and fire management.

Beyond the campsite – considering some of the enjoyable diversions on offer to the successful canoe camper who has made it somewhere a little wild.

How to stay safe – ways to look after yourself on the journey and around the campsite.

Measurements

Many of the canoes we use come from North America, where they still use feet and inches to describe all dimensions. As the habit seems to be maintained over here too, at least with canoes, I will continue to employ these old imperial measurements when discussing them. Keen to avoid confusion though, and because I'm well aware that many readers may be understandably baffled by all this archaic stuff, I will also provide decimal versions in brackets.

Who this book is for

Regardless of what our European ancestors may have got up to in the past, canoe camping as we know and practise it today is principally a North American phenomenon – and a significant body of impressive published advice is already available for the Canadian and US paddler. While I hope that a prospective canoe camper living anywhere in the world will find plenty of useful advice within the covers of this book, the content does have a distinct European if not British slant. This is inevitable. It is where I canoe and camp after all. So while I don't mention the problems of dealing with a resident grizzly bear population for example, I will cover Scottish midges, Swedish mosquitoes and issues specific to European access.

This book is also produced from another particular perspective. If the average Minnesotan or inhabitant of Ontario or Quebec is asked about canoe camping, they will have a very definite activity in mind. For the North American, canoe camping means heading into the wild. I share that view.

Much as I relish any chance to put up a tent at the end of a canoe journey, it is the opportunity to paddle off in search of somewhere as remote and unspoilt as possible that holds the strongest appeal. Wild camping, or putting up a tent up somewhere out of the way and unregulated at the end of a canoe journey, is the activity that forms the principal subject for discussion in the following chapters.

The opportunities to wild camp in the more populated parts of Europe are somewhat limited. It is far from easy for the UK paddler, and not really possible for anyone paddling south of the Scottish border. This being the case, mention will be made of the use of formal waterside campsites – but that mention will be brief. My eyes and thoughts will be drawn to the far empty horizon. It is hoped that those drawn to open this book will understand.

A final comment regarding brands. Having worked my way through a large body of camping kit, rejecting much of it along the way, I feel I am now in the very privileged position of owning products from some of the best camping gear manufacturers out there. If I mention a brand, it is because I trust it, and want others to have the chance to share the benefits. I hasten to add though that I'm not sponsored or paid by any of these companies (although some do ask me to test or review their kit), and hope that this independence confers added validity to any comments I make.

Of course we canoeists are blessed.

Letting your canoe take the strain.

What To Take

Unlike the rugged backpacker, or even the cycle-tourer, the canoeist can almost forget about restricting camping kit to essentials. With a suitable canoe pulled up on the bank or beach, those days of laying out everything you'd like to take, before immediately producing a large pile of rejected items, are now all but past. If you want to take something in particular, there's probably room, even for the kitchen sink – well at least a large plastic bowl. Nor do you need to think small. After all, the canoe was designed from the start for haulage. It seems only fitting then to let it continue in that role. What this means in practice, is that not only can you let your canoe take the strain, but when it comes to selecting what to take, that impressive carrying capacity and space provides plenty of options.

Of course seasoned campers may feel they have a pretty good idea about what to take already, but using a canoe really does change things. You might even find yourself surprised by what can now be carried into the wild. So for everyone new to the wonderful world of canoe camping, including the old camping hands, welcome to the 'kit' section.

Before I make a proper start, I do want to make a bit of a point about choice. What follows is largely a description of the items that Susannah and I choose to take canoe camping. It's what suits us. It is not a 'must have' list, an inventory that you should feel compelled to follow to the letter, but a collection of suggestions. If you don't care much for headtorches for example, and even after experiencing my enthusiasm you'd still prefer a hand-held version, then that should be the illumination for you.

Everything you need for a cold weather camping trip. And yes, it really will all go in.

Nor should you feel constrained by the list's perhaps rather Spartan limits. Despite the load-hauling capacity of the canoe I still prefer to keep things relatively simple, carrying only the minimum I consider necessary to ensure, or at least enhance, the likelihood of comfort. That doesn't mean you have to follow suit. So long as you're not impinging on anyone else's pleasure, or harming any of that lovely but sensitive wild stuff you'll enjoy finding out there, you should be able to take what you want. If you appreciate the comfort of camping chairs, or the entertainment offered by a chess board, please take them.

Enjoyment and comfort is the aim with all this. As long ago as the 1880s, the woodsman George Sears was railing against any inherent expectation of having to 'rough it' while canoe camping. He considered that there was quite enough involved in the artificial stresses and strains of life in the towns and cities. I agree. Camping, particularly camping while supported by a canoe, should be almost the opposite of roughing it. That, in essence, is what this book is about.

On reaching the end of this section, those of you with canoe camping experience may feel that I have overlooked something or other. It is also inevitable that along the way I will dismiss someone's cherished camping method, item or technique. Where this happens, I hope I will at least give a considered reason why.

And last of all, I may well have it wrong – at least about some things. Until a few years ago I was convinced, for example, that the traditional foam bedroll was all I needed to sleep on. In fact, I hadn't even bothered with one of those for a decade or two. Since being introduced to their wonders however, it is now highly unlikely that you will find me nestling down to sleep at night without a self-inflating Thermarest mattress between me and the seemingly ever more lumpy world. I continue to learn – I hope.

Very basic canoe camping.

Essentials

I recall one very satisfying, still summer night when, on a whim, we decided to sleep at the top edge of a sandy beach, sheltered only by our upturned canoe. We had sleeping bags, mats and simple cooking gear, but that was it. I mention this as an immediate reminder that no activity as uplifting as canoe camping should be bound by convention.

For almost every other canoe camping trip it is worth carrying a little more kit, and there are a fair number of things you should probably consider taking every time. Here then is the list. It comes with what I hope are useful comments, and some thoughts about alternatives. As any guidance on what to do with it all (packing, protection, stowage aboard your canoe, and use) will be fairly lengthy, this information is provided in later chapters. As a quick reference, and possible checklist, a simplified inventory is provided in an appendix (see page 217).

Tents

It is almost inevitable when considering camping kit that most thought will be given to this temporary shelter, and quite rightly so. Yet while you might expect me to now embark on a long and carefully argued case for one particular type of tent or another, I'm tempted at first to do just about the opposite. Put simply, if you already own a tent, and assuming it's reasonably well made of course, then you should use that.

Good tents are far from cheap after all. If you've already parted with what is likely to be a considerable sum, and you're happy with the result, I'd far rather see it stowed in a canoe and propelled somewhere interesting, than have you postpone this happy event until the 'right' accommodation is found for the job. Perhaps unsurprisingly, I do have a few thoughts and opinions on the matter, and you won't need to read that much further to encounter them, but to begin with, don't be put off using what you have.

Assuming though that you aren't already the happy owner of a decent tent, what then are the key considerations?

Well, worrying about size shouldn't be one of them. Manufacturers have spent vast amounts of time and research funds in an attempt to perfect the backpacking or

Canoe camping tents come in all shapes and sizes.

mountain tent – as roomy and as strong as possible, but still luggable. Yet, wonderful as many of these shelters are, they inevitably represent a compromise, with pretty cramped accommodation. If you end up with much more than a few centimetres of space around your sleeping mat at night you're doing well.

Cyclists able to let their vehicle do the donkeywork can allow their tent can grow a little. Those taking to the water in a kayak may manage something a touch larger again. But it is when the canoe is deployed to venture into the wild that camping can be elevated to proper outdoor living. The reason? Well I've already mentioned it – the carrying capacity of the canoe itself.

Plenty of space for even a fairly large tent (and stove).

In addition to Susannah and myself, our 16ft (4.9m) canoe can transport hundreds of kilograms of kit. Suddenly the size and weight of a tent is of little real concern. It's possible to take almost anything you like – even a small marquee. Just remember that you'll end up carrying it yourself at some point, possibly over some distance.

Pretty much the only limiting factor is the stowage space, and that's not much of a restriction. For the sake of good canoe paddling trim (large tents are usually quite heavy), load security, and other canoe packing inclinations that I'll mention later, I prefer to stow at least part of our tent beneath the rear thwart (see page 74 to show you where to find this thwart, and page 104 for canoe packing advice). This under thwart space means a maximum packed tent girth of a little over 30cm (around 12 to 13ins).

In the event, with almost 60cm (two feet) of canoe beam (width) available here, it is possible to squeeze something a little wider into shape to fit, but if you work on the principle that you have something in the region of 30 x 40 x 80cm (12 x 15 x 32ins) available, it's clear that you can still take a pretty big tent. Something with a packed weight of as much as 15kg (30lbs) can be carried with ease. Of course, if really determined, an even bigger shelter can be loaded in the unrestricted space between the thwarts, or split and loaded in two parts, even two canoes. I imagine though that the dimensions listed here will give scope for even the most ambitious campsite architect.

Then it's down to design and materials.

For us, the criteria for the perfect canoe camping tent includes bomb-proof construction (in a material that can be repaired easily in the field should something go wrong), excellent foul weather characteristics, and plenty of room to stand and move about. Ease and speed of pitching, preferably single-handed, is important, and the ability to cook under cover is also a very high priority. In brief, we are looking for space, versatility, and quality of design and construction. Quite a tall order.

Older readers may recall the canvas ridge and bell tents from Scouting or Guiding days. Although definitely embraced within the 'traditional' bracket, both are still available today. Considering the work involved in producing one, and the cost of good canvas, some of the prices advertised are pretty reasonable too. When well made, these tried and tested tents are a joy. I certainly miss my old greying ridge tent, which long ago succumbed to advanced age and a hard life.

I tend to fret a bit if shut away from the environment I've paddled out to connect with. Even when the view is a touch wet and blustery our tent flap rarely closes

The only surviving picture of my old ridge tent, at an archaeological dig – much missed, and now long gone.

before dark, sometimes not even then. This is where the ridge tent excels. Both ends can be opened if the weather is still. Even when things take an interesting turn for the worse, you can still leave the downwind end exposed, allowing an excellent chance to watch all the meteorological fun. In good weather, the sides of both the ridge and traditional bell tents can be lifted completely, leaving only an excellent sun awning. All in all then, these tried and tested forms of tent offer plenty of versatility, and very pleasing canoe camping tent options. Versions can still be purchased either in traditional canvas or more modern materials.

A modern canvas bell tent.

When it comes to providing views, it is unlikely that the 'Baker' tent (also known as the 'campfire' or 'reflector' tent), so beloved of many Canadian canoe camping families, could easily be beaten. If you want a camping room with a view, this style of tent, with its open front, will almost certainly not disappoint. I say almost certainly, as I've not used one myself, at least not a purpose-built example, and can only replicate the often very positive comments from those that have.

My only criticism of all these traditional tents concerns the effort and time required to pitch them. I've had plenty of experience with both ridge and bell style tents, and can even raise one on my own if pushed, but I'll also be the first to acknowledge that the job is much easier with help. Fine of course if you intend to camp with others, less convenient for the lone explorer. As admitted, I haven't put up a Baker tent, and while well aware that these have often been pitched single-handed, the job could surely never be described as quick and easy, at least not compared to some of the shelters now available.

Which brings us to our current shelter.

After considerable research, trial and deliberation, one tent stood out, for us at least, and we've been using a Tentipi Safir 7 very happily for a few years now. Not cheap it is true, and certainly not small for two campers either, but no problem for our canoe, and I can put up this well-designed tipi on my own in a matter of minutes (far faster in fact than any other larger tent design I've come across – old or new). Now Susannah and I enjoy as much excellent tent space as we like.

Our tipi, and an April dawn on the edge of Loch Etive, Scotland.

Like the traditional ridge, bell or Baker tent, the Tentipi will need a groundsheet. An excellent purpose-made version can be bought, at quite a price, but something perfectly serviceable can be provided at relatively little cost by purchasing a tarpaulin, either canvas or synthetic. A plastic version will certainly be cheaper, and if kept clear of anything hot, makes a totally waterproof floor.

One drawback to a tipi-style tent is that it can be hard to enjoy a view in bad weather. With angled sides, the doorway, if left open, is rather exposed to the elements – and it's not particularly large anyway (although one door-side peg can be unhooked and an extra tent panel folded back successfully, with little impact on stability).

Use of an additional porch helps with a tipi, but I tend to just put up with the rain getting in at the door. These tents are large enough after all, and this small damp area really doesn't impinge significantly on the usable space.

And as I've mentioned space a few times, I would encourage all prospective canoe campers to think big, at least to some extent. There is nothing, for example, quite like being able to stand up in a tent. Not so important perhaps in good sunny weather, but the appeal grows quickly once the rain sets in for a while.

Which is the time when it becomes really quite important to be able to cook inside your temporary home, or at least under its cover somewhere. Much as we might wish to enjoy every aspect of the outdoors, there is little fun in being forced outside a small tent in prolonged bad weather to produce a meal over an exposed stove or fire. It is at these times that a tent fitted either with a good awning or porch, or big enough and designed specifically to allow cooking inside, is invaluable.

With care and common sense you can use a gas or liquid-fuel stove in even quite a small tent, but this isn't much fun, and I'm afraid I've seen the results of getting it wrong. The bigger the tent the better, and safer, especially when it is purpose built to take a fire or stove beneath its welcome shelter.

With its huge awning the Baker tent shelters an open fire perfectly. Not surprising of course, as long ago that's exactly what it was designed to do. Like the ridge and bell tent, it can also manage a wood-fired stove – so long as an appropriate fire-proof flue vent setup is used (often available from the tent or stove manufacturer). In my book this is pretty important, and tents such as these, or the Tentipi of course, designed from the outset to shelter either an open or stove-enclosed wood fire, will always form my preferred canoe camping shelter. Tents that are purpose-built for internal wood-fired stove use, are also likely to have built in ventilation, essential to help avoid the potential build up of dangerous carbon monoxide gas. Never use a stove of any sort in a tent that isn't set up for, or doesn't allow, the movement of plenty of fresh air.

While on this subject, tent materials themselves are worth some consideration. Although modern synthetic tent fabrics can be treated with fire retardant chemicals, anything that is derived essentially from oil is always going to possess certain rather worrying characteristics. And while the sensible use of a nylon or similar tent

Breakfast on the beach.

Taking the opportunity to dry out a canvas tent.

should cause no real concern if the fire is kept outside and well away, the inbuilt fire resistant benefits of a canvas shelter are worth mentioning, or even stressing. If you are determined, you can set light to a tent made from cotton of course, particularly if it has been treated to keep out rain, but it is harder.

What is more, a canvas tent is far more resistant to the insidious damage caused by sparks. These little hole-melting projectiles are almost inevitable around a campfire, and can ruin a 'plastic' tent in a matter of minutes if you're unlucky.

Mind you, if you do choose canvas, just make sure that it's fully dry before packing it away, at least when you've finally finished with it. Plastic tents don't much like to stay damp for long either, but cotton really will succumb to terminal rot very quickly if stored in company with any moisture.

My last word concerns mosquito nets. If your tent is modern it may well have one built in, at least to cover the entrances. If not, you will almost certainly need to add something in the warmer months, especially in Scotland and Scandinavia. Nets come in many shapes and sizes, so there shouldn't be any trouble finding one that suits. It should also be borne in mind that Scottish midges, which are surprisingly small, can often nip through the holes in a standard mosquito net with ease.

Small tents (and tarps)

Having gone on a little about the benefits of using a large tent, there are times, occasionally, when they may not offer the best option. Big tents provide many advantages, but only when there's space to put one up.

At the end of a fulfilling and uplifting day of exploration, with shoulders aching, you are probably looking forward to no more than pitching a tent, lighting a quick fire, eating and then falling asleep. I recall pushing our way up against the varied flow of the River Laisälven in Sweden on one of those days, growing a little desperate. The forest cover was so dense, or the bank so boggy, we could find nothing to cater for a tent for miles – or our tent at least. On this occasion we did find somewhere eventually, pulling ashore to pitch our tipi in a tiny bank-side clearing, but identifying somewhere for a small tent would have been much easier. If you are heading anywhere new, up an unexplored (for you at least) river or along a rarely-visited lake, it might well be worth carrying a small tent as well. Many backpacking shelters measure little more than a stored sleeping bag. It wouldn't be hard to carry one – just in case.

On the rare occasions when space has been at a premium, a small tent had always saved the day. Then we met the Muonionjoki, a river forming the border between Sweden and Finland.

Long sections of lively and shallow rapids lay above and below us, neither of which we fancied dealing with that late in the day. Admittedly, we still had a fairly lengthy stretch of easily-paddled river to choose from, but the banks running along both shores were steep, narrow and covered in bushes. No room for our tipi here. The problem was, the banks were far too steep even for our small tent.

This is where I first mention tarpaulins, or 'tarps'. At first I didn't include these versatile fabric sheets in the essentials list, relegating them to the 'sensible additions'

A small tent. Plenty of room for this one, or a big tent, but space isn't always available for the larger version.

section, but the more I considered these simple items of kit, the more I doubted my choice. Even if they aren't exactly vital, they come close enough to creep in under the 'essential' heading.

So, back on the banks of the Muonionjoki, with a simple pine-branch platform propped on stones to provide a level sleeping area, and an absolutely essential mosquito net pegged up under our outspread tarp, we could finally sleep.

Even when you have room for your tent the tarp can be indispensible. A lot depends on the tent you choose to take in the first place, and the smaller your principal shelter, the greater the potential benefits of a tarp.

All this awning stuff is discussed further under 'Dealing with wet' on page 161. At this point I will make do by stressing only that something which can be strung up to provide shelter in prolonged bad weather can be very welcome, particularly if your tent is too small to spend any amount of time inside with any degree of enjoyment.

Ideally your tarp will be relatively heavy duty, although if well secured, even a very lightweight fabric awning will do. Overall size will depend on the number of people you hope to shelter, but something with minimum dimensions of 2m x 3m should be considered, with 3m x 4m or more being a better bet.

Try to either purchase or make a sheet that has plenty of tough eyelets around the edge for guy ropes. Some form of looped attachment at the centre, with lots of reinforcement to cope with the inevitable strain, is very helpful, allowing a rain-shedding tent shape of some sort to be produced. A good supply of guy rope material (light rope or cord) will also be invaluable.

Finally, if a mosquito net is useful with a tent, the importance of adding one to any tarp sleeping setup should be obvious.

Using a tarp to provide shelter on the Swedish side of the Muonionjoki.

Sleeping kit

Little, other than the sun, can improve a good day outside quite as much as a decent sleep the night before.

Sleeping bags

You may well own a sleeping bag already. It might have your full confidence. If not, it would probably be a good idea to consider whether it's actually up to the job. Sadly, there are many totally inadequate offerings out there masquerading as proper sleeping bags, fit only for children's sleepovers, or the warmest summer festival night. Unless your bag still looks convincing after reading the following discussion, a new one may be the safest option. Being miserable is the best you can hope for if sleeping somewhere slightly wild in the wrong model.

If you do need to buy a new sleeping bag, and while there are decisions to be made with regard to expected temperature ranges and conditions, the principal choice is going to be between two forms of insulation – down or synthetic.

Sleeping bags, and other sleeping kit.

In summary, down-filled bags are usually far lighter and pack smaller than their synthetic counterparts, but cost a lot more and have a worrying tendency to not work at all well if they get wet (all the light, fluffy, heat-trapping, feathery filaments collapse and stick together).

To my mind this decision has been made a lot harder by the increased quality of synthetic-filled bags. Go back a few years, and even after the extra cost and rather poor wet weather characteristics of a down bag were taken into account, the decision was still pretty simple, or at least I always thought so. Expensive yes, but so long as a down-filled bag was kept dry, the benefits of these light, small-packing and very warm bags far overshadowed the often dubious qualities of a synthetic version.

Now though, synthetic bags are ever lighter and more compressible. And with packed size and weight also not a problem for a canoe camper, they make a very good alternative. Sleeping bags filled with something synthetic really are also a lot cheaper than down-filled versions, some of which can put quite a dent in any bank balance.

In the end, I still prefer a down filling, but possibly only because I can't help associating it with luxury. After years spent lying in some heavy, clumpy and usually rather chilly synthetic-filled bags, dreaming of the day when I could finally purchase one of these feathery camping gems, I'm not going to give up my down bags now I own one or two.

Next up when making a decision about a new sleeping bag is the temperature in which you are likely to be camping. These bags have to cater for trips into every environment from the jungle to one of the two poles, and a bag designed to keep you alive amongst the ice floes at -30°C, is not going to be much fun on the shore of Loch Maree in August. Neither will that skimpy jungle bag do much for a night's sleep anywhere in Britain just after New Year.

If you pick up a sleeping bag in a shop, a label is usually attached somewhere with a great swathe of additional temperature related information. This is the industry standard information, resulting from strict laboratory tests. The prevailing system in Europe (using what is called the EN13537 standard) is a little odd, and provides the following information (which I reproduce only in an attempt to reduce confusion):

an **upper limit**, which is the highest temperature at which a 'standard' adult male is considered able to have a comfortable night's sleep;

a **comfort rating**, based on a the lowest temperature at which it is thought a 'standard' adult female will have a contented night's sleep;

a **lower limit**, based on the lowest temperature at which a 'standard' adult male is deemed to be able to have a comfy night's sleep; and

an **extreme rating**, or survival rating for a 'standard' adult male. This is an extreme survival temperature rating only. It is way below the point at which any comfort can be expected.

Still confused? I'm not surprised.

As an initial guide, something that caters for an expected minimum temperature between the comfort and lower limit, is a good purchase.

Fortunately, most sleeping bag retailers recognise the need for campers to be able to identify the right bag for the job. They are probably also aware that the industry standard information isn't always of much help. Catalogues, shops and online outlets often divide their wares into sensible, almost universally recognised, groups. These use a season-based system, resulting in:

- One-season bags (summer only)
- Two-season (late spring, summer and early autumn)
- Three-season (anything but winter use)
- Four-season (as the name suggests, designed for action all year).

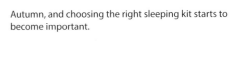
Autumn, and choosing the right sleeping kit starts to become important.

You may also come across bags described as ready for 4+ season use, but unless you plan on canoe camping in Antarctica these probably aren't for you.

When it comes to sleeping preferences, and tolerances to discomfort, everyone is different. Specific advice is made yet more tricky by recognised variations, even if only slight, in the way manufacturers present their ratings, but here goes. For most British winter use, even in Scotland, a four-season bag will do (with an EN13537 'lower limit' of perhaps -9°C to -12°C). Women should note that the industry recognises that they usually need a warmer bag. Some may find this offering a little warm in all but the harshest conditions, but will certainly welcome the benefits when the temperatures really drop. For British summer use a two-season bag will cater for the odd chilly night. A lower rating of perhaps 0°C for England and Wales and -2°C for Scotland will suffice. Three-season bags make good all-rounders, with lower limits at about -7°C (please note the *about*) catering for all but the coldest months or locations.

Some of the better manufacturers try to help further, and Mountain Equipment for example, include a 'recommended sleepzone' on the label for each bag. My winter bag reads +10°C to -9°C, while my all-purpose choice suggests +20°C to -5°C. Very helpful.

An alternative to dealing with temperature variations is the layering option. This does require a fair bit of financial outlay, and best suits those who have been buying sleeping bags gently over many years. It goes like this. Start with a thin summer-weight version, and then, as temperatures drop, simply pull on another loose bag. I'm lucky, and tend to sleep warm. Even in the coldest British weather, one good winter or 'four-season' grade bag is usually fine. But when the frost lies deep and even, Susannah has been known to lurk within as many as three down bags before now.

The sleeping bag layering system in use (only two this time).

Three other advances have helped keep down bags high on my preferred kit list – two connected with the bag itself, the last related to storage. Each aspect deals with the problems of damp, as mentioned, that curse of down bags.

There is something particularly depressing about a wet down sleeping bag. Depending on the conditions in which you are camping, there is also something potentially very dangerous. Those involved in serious cold weather exploration are sometimes given this advice – *"If you are heading to where a wet down bag means you die, take a synthetic one."* A bit extreme perhaps, and unlikely to be a concern for the average canoe camper, but it makes a clear point.

Fortunately, those talented design boffins are now producing some very clever outer materials for down sleeping bags. Some of the more expensive examples are fully waterproof, and yet still breathe properly. Various water resistant Pertex coverings are almost as good, and a fair bit cheaper. My current down bag, made by the renowned British company Mountain Equipment, has a Pertex shell (outer fabric), and shrugs off the odd encounter with a little rain (I did mention that I like to leave the tent flap open).

The other recent technological advance is the waterproofing of the down itself, before it ends up in the bag. This is all very new, and having not tried it myself, all I can say is that positive reactions have been heard from those that have. If it does work, and real-life field use should tell us soon, this would be a rather wonderful advance.

Prevention will always be better than cure though, and this is where dry bags are first mentioned. I have a bit of a thing about these little camping wonders, which are discussed further on page 95. At this point I intend only to say that the use of a good dry bag to transport your sleeping bag has made the choice of a down filling so much more sensible.

My last suggestion with all this tricky sleeping bag choice – if you aren't fortunate to have experienced outdoor types as friends – is to visit a good shop. Balanced advice should always be available from your local camping and outdoor gear store. If it isn't on offer, go elsewhere. Staff in a good outlet will do their best to ensure that you make the most of your time outside. Just tell them what you need your bag for, where you intend to use it, and when, and they'll be able to help. As the writer of a guide, this suggestion may seem to be something of a cop-out, an evasion of responsibility, but I'm sure the only real dereliction of duty would be to avoid offering this sound advice.

Sleeping mats

Despite roughing it for many years without any sleeping mat, the advantages of one in terms of comfort and warmth far outweigh any piffling concerns over additional weight or required stowage. A decent sleeping mat surely represents a must-have item.

Any form of good mat not only provides a huge amount of additional comfort (the ground doesn't seem to grow any softer or less lumpy over the years), but also acts as a very important thermal barrier between you and what you're lying on. Despite the efforts of a good sleeping bag, the ground will almost literally suck the warmth from you without something insulating in between. In fact, most sleeping bag manufacturers assume the use of a decent mat when designing and grading their products.

Foam mats (so long as they use closed cell foam materials that don't soak up water) make a great step forward in the search for sleeping satisfaction. And then...

Thermarest mats have already cropped up. They don't have to come from this dependable manufacturer of course, but something in the thin, self-inflating line is worth its weight in dry wood. Some are even designed for two friendly campers, and quite a few have down insulation inside.

These lovely things can transform a night's sleep under canvas. I didn't know what I was missing, but would now put up quite a fight if someone came after mine in the night.

Pillows

Which brings us to another little night time comfort that I certainly never considered when dragging oversized rucksacks up hills and mountains – pillows (see the sleeping bag 'layering' photo). Even as I write this I know that some readers will be

Sleeping mats in action – their supporting role you might say.

In weather like this, using dry bags to transport sleeping kit is vital.

shaking their heads and tutting, but if this is your reaction, may I encourage you to think again.

My hope is that everyone reading this book will sally forth to reap the bounties available to the canoe camper. All this enjoyment is so much more likely, and significantly enhanced, if you aren't tired. If you choose to use a pillow at home to ensure a decent night's sleep (and I suspect all but a very few will), why not do the same wherever you decide to pitch a tent. You have the space in your canoe after all. My pillows (yes two) are even filled with goose down.

Stoves

This section is split to cover stoves for cooking on, and stoves that heat tents – which you should be able to cook on too.

Cooking stoves

A tiny and very efficient canister gas stove. Great for the backpacker, but you don't need to restrict yourself to this.

Assuming you are considering a purpose-built camping stove, designed and constructed by a leading outdoor manufacturer, your choice is likely to be efficient, robust and reliable. Almost all will do a perfectly good job.

Most backpacking stoves run on some form of bottled (canister) gas. The only real issue then is to ensure that you have enough spare canisters – and that they are full. I do recall once shoving about half a dozen little metal containers into a rucksack, knowing that none was quite full, but assuming that between them all I would find enough fuel to cook a meal. Of course I was miles from anywhere before I sat, cold and hungry in a very treeless environment, shaking one canister after another, my mood darkening with each attempt. Something vaguely warm was eventually produced.

Many perfectly decent stoves run on liquid fuels too of course, some able to use just about anything vaguely combustible. Be prepared to pay a reasonable sum for a recognised model from a good manufacturer such as MSR or Primus, at which point you are unlikely to go wrong.

Nevertheless, even the best of these small stoves can sometimes be a little moody, and as they are designed with weight reduction in mind, they can also be a touch fragile. While the practicalities of a mountain ascent may restrict you to just one tiny stove, there is no need to skimp here. When expecting to cook with gas I usually take two, just to be on the safe side. I also try to remember to carry spare parts such as pipes, tubing or O-ring seals.

Remember though that you don't need to focus on just the smaller stove offerings in the shop.

In almost all cases, the stove designed for climbers and backpackers will do for the canoe camper, but like the mountain or backpacking tent, they come with inbuilt compromises. To save weight, all components are reduced to the smallest size that will still perform, just. Burner areas, stabilising feet, hose lengths, etc., will all be as tiny as possible. The average camping stove intended for human-powered travel will fit in your hand. I've just weighed mine. It comes in at a precise 91g (just over 3oz). Even with a canister of fuel, it's less weighty than a tin of beans. Great if intended for a rucksack, but the carrying capacity of your canoe means that you have the luxury to look a little wider.

In fact some of the smaller stoves designed for car haulage will not be too big. When expecting to employ a gas stove, we ship the double-ring burner that usually sits in our van. This comes with a 3.9kg gas bottle on the end of a yard or two of rubber hose. You might spot the orange bottle in a couple of campsite photos.

Tent stoves

Wood-fired tent stoves keep you warm. Just as importantly when planning to go camping on the north-west fringe of Europe, they also keep you dry. There is nothing quite like the luxury of being able to rid damp clothes of that cold clammy feel. Pick a good stove and a tent becomes a home. So what makes a good canoe camping tent stove?

In brief, something that possesses that tricky balance between strength and light weight. Of course it should also pack down small enough to fit in your canoe, for while I have made quite a deal about the haulage capabilities of your craft, there are limits.

Assuming you are a dab hand with angle grinders, tin-snips and pop-riveters, much fun can be had making your own stove, and I once had a little beauty made from an old gas bottle. Fortunately, for those without a welder in the shed, there are some very good professionally manufactured models out there, so anyone should be able to put their hands on something usable, if they can afford it.

A canoe-sized gas stove.

Cooking on our Eldfell stove.

Tent, Eldfell stove and canoe in Scotland.

While there are exceptions (one or two notable ones), good tent stoves don't tend to be cheap, at least not ones that can readily be dropped into a canoe. Much of this is down to weight, with anything relatively inexpensive, usually being commensurately heavy, and vice versa.

Ideally, your chosen stove should weigh no more than about 15kg (35lbs). Maximum packed measurements will need to be in the region of 30 x 40 x 75cm (12 x 15 x 30ins), the size limited by the space available to stow it in your canoe below the thwarts (see page 104 for canoe packing advice).

Clever stove designs allow the chimney to be broken down into sections, sometimes packed inside the body of the stove itself. If not, a single length chimney can usually be shipped in one piece. The firebox should be as large as possible, baffled to encourage the heat to stay inside and fitted with a good air control system. It should also have a decent hotplate for a pan or two.

If asked to pick out one stove that fits the bill, I have to mention our Eldfell, made by Tentipi. It is light, tough and effective, but also rather scarily expensive. Less costly options are available, and something called the Frontier stove looks very interesting. This has been designed with disaster relief and humanitarian situations in mind, and comes at a very reasonable price (and weight). My experience of these stoves is limited, but I suspect that anyone working to something of a budget would do well with this choice.

Cooking and eating kit

So much of this must be down to personal preference, but the following discussion offers some suggestions, based on our experiences. I'd like to think that these days we usually get it somewhere near right. In fact, what follows is pretty much an inventory of what we would take on the average trip.

Cooking

One standard frying pan and a nesting set of three stainless steel MSR pots. Between them these cater for most of our cooking needs. We also usually carry a fairly big cast iron lidded pot. This is heavy it's true, but superior in so many ways when cooking that we don't mind. With the lid, it is also very versatile, providing somewhere to roast and bake if needed – in effect a small Dutch oven.

As the MSR pots have those separate aluminium clamp handles, one of these will always be found lurking within the inside pot – I hope. To stop the handle rattling around in there I wrap it in a plastic carrier bag, even interleaving others between the pots for the same reason. Not only does this keep things quiet, but those bags can cover a multitude of jobs, from rubbish bags to somewhere to store freshly collected mussels. Then, because it is so easy to lose or break things, another pot clamp goes into our eating kit bag.

To supplement these cooking vessels we carry a small Primus kettle to boil water for drinks when a fire is going (big enough for two cups). For all the times when there isn't something crackling away merrily, we also ship a large stainless steel Kelly Kettle. This has seen so much action that I've burnt the bottom out of the fire base and had to make an emergency outdoor repair with a circle of beaten corrugated iron. I originally intended to replace this, but it seems to do the job and hasn't fallen out yet. This wonderful piece of kit provides boiling water quickly, and free. All you need is dry twigs, grass, or even nettle stems.

Thoughts then turn to all the odds and ends that make cooking in the wild pleasurable without overloading your trusty canoe. Perhaps this bit is best presented as a list:

- A good knife – it is often best, for health and practicality, to have a dedicated cutting implement for cooking.

- A chopping board – not essential, but a board does make life much easier. We have a fairly large, but very thin and light plastic board. More of a sheet really, and highly recommended.

- Tin foil – has many uses and is reusable.

- Kitchen roll.

- A can and bottle opener – depending on how you like to take your food. A Swiss Army knife stashed somewhere amongst your kit makes a good backup when the opener you need can't be found.

- A wooden spoon and/or spatula – you can make your own on site of course, but it is useful to start out with something ready-made.

- Washing up liquid – preferably biodegradable. There are some very handy bottles of 'do everything' detergent available. These can wash anything from your hair to your hat, including the dirty bowls, yet still break down into something we're led to believe is OK once released into the environment.

- Matches – you just can't have too many boxes secreted at various dry (more of this on page 95) points throughout your kit. Carry a fire steel if you wish. I do, partly because it doesn't suffer from damp. I even use it sometimes, but you will do best to invest in matches. Please don't feel bad about carrying a gas lighter as well if you wish. I'd far rather have a range of fire lighting kit available than to worry about being accused of neglecting traditional skills. You don't need to be able to produce a blaze with an old Viking fire steel and the nearest pebble to be a proper camper. If you can, then great, it may even come in useful one day, but I'd argue that always being able to put your hand on a dry box of matches demonstrates greater canoe camping skills.

Because I have a liking for wood fires, we carry a pair of fire irons (their use is discussed on page 152). These provide pretty essential pot supports. A pair of steel road pins will do (those lengths of mild steel rod with a point at one end and a curly bit at the other, usually used to support temporary fencing), but angle iron is far better, being much more stable in use (60–80cm lengths of 20mm x 20mm x 3mm mild steel work well). We also carry a couple of old oven shelves, the chromed wire sort. Used either on their own, or laid over the fire irons, these provide a useful surface for grilling, or just making toast.

As they help provide fuel, I also tend to see an axe and saw as part of the cooking kit, I'll come back to all this fire and cooking stuff, including axe and saw use, later (page 137), but the selection of these vital tools deserves almost immediate attention, and a dedicated section follows below.

Camp kitchen kit.
Clockwise from bottom left – Washing up bowl, cloths, scourer and universal 'clean everything' biodegradable detergent; cutting board, spatula, tin opener and knife; frying pan and wooden spoon; MSR pans (and handle); Kelly Kettle; Primus kettle; and fire irons and wire oven shelf.

An axe and bow saw – essential items if you plan to cook over an open fire.

Eating kit. Plastic bowls (large and small), mugs, and assorted sporks.

Employing an open fire, our cast iron pot can be used like a Dutch oven to bake and roast, but anyone keen to try baking at the campsite might consider buying a reflector oven. I haven't used one of these since Scouting days, but with care and practice they work well. A very fine looking version is produced by the Swedish company Svante. Made in aluminium, this folds flat and weighs less than 1 kg.

Eating

Anyone who has spotted my preference for woolly jumpers and cotton smocks may suspect that I'm a bit of a traditionalist, likely to head into the wild with nothing but a tin mug, an enamel plate and a large knife. What they may have missed is my equal liking for Gore-Tex and quick-drying trousers. In short, I like things that work, and when it comes to what to eat off, or eat with, I do like plastic. Using a plastic mug is so much better than losing the skin off your lips to a scalding tin mug – one piece of camping kit I will try to avoid. Even fingers aren't safe from these little monsters.

To accompany our mugs, two plastic bowls, one large, one small, and a spork will be packed for each of us. Bowls are so much more useful than a plate when surfaces are uneven. I do hate the sight of a good meal lying on the ground. While we often just take a fork and spoon from the kitchen, sporks are versatile, very light and relatively cheap. I suspect I may have about six (which is sensible, as they do break). You can even buy large ones to stir bubbling pots of food.

The other essential is a good knife. This is the first mention of what must be one of the most important pieces of canoe camping kit. Please don't be put off by the utterly misinformed rantings of the modern political classes. A knife is a tool, a vital tool. It is no more a weapon than a length of wood, both of which only become a problem in the hands of an idiot. Carry a sensible knife and it will improve your experience of the wild repeatedly. Without wishing to become too sensationalist, it might even save your life one day. Much more about this vital implement on page 47.

Returning to less controversial subjects …

Food

Of course all that cooking and eating kit is a bit redundant without some food.

This is where personal preference really comes into play, but perhaps it is possible to break down the styles of food likely to be loaded aboard your canoe into two broad categories, basic ingredients and pre-prepared meals. Some prefer to stick to either one group or the other. In all likelihood your victuals will be a mix of the two, but what to take and what mix?

Tins of food make cooking simple, are easy to carry, but fairly heavy. They are also still just as bulky when empty (until you stamp on them – wearing a good tough boot that is). What you find inside those tins ranges from the inedible – in my book at least – to some surprisingly impressive fare. Cost and quality seem to be fairly closely linked in these matters. These days it is possible to find a wide range of pre-cooked meals in plastic sachets. Some of the expensive ones aren't too bad, although often surprisingly salty. Dried meals are also available in sachets, and I

The canoe camping kitchen.

admit to having no experience of them whatsoever. I have seen other people eat them mind you, confirming my intention to leave it that way.

Given the chance, Susannah and I have a definite preference for cooking from scratch. When conditions allow, and that seems to be most of the time, we usually manage to produce something we're happy with, starting with basic ingredients.

Many vegetables such as onions, potatoes and carrots will last for days, even weeks if you're lucky enough to be out there that long. Even the shorter-lived varieties will probably survive in an edible state until the end of your trip. Not everyone will want to follow suit, but garlic always finds its way into our vegetable collection (and some claim it helps keep mosquitoes at bay). Fruit is a little less durable, but apples are always a good standby with a reasonable shelf life. Some meat and dairy products will last a surprisingly long time if kept somewhere cool and dark. This usually isn't that difficult to achieve. Many fridges hover at around 5°C, and in winter you might look forward to days this warm.

An example of what we might take for a few days in the wild. This collection includes a few cans, UHT milk, cartons of fruit juice, eggs, cheese and chorizo, the remains of a loaf, fresh vegetables, crispbread, then flour, oats, pasta and rice (with dry bags or waterproof containers), a dried meal in a sealed box, a few bottles of pasta sauce, cooking oil, concentrated tomato sauce, pepper, soy sauce, instant coffee, teabags (in their own sealed box), and some biscuits. There is also a bottle of water (just in case) and some may notice a box of matches.

At sunnier times of year, the use of some form of insulated bag or box will usually see things stay fresh for quite a few days. Just try to remember to keep it in the shade. If your 'cold' food container is waterproof, why not sit it in the nearest stream or lake edge if things really hot up.

For the few days that most of us will spend in the wild at any one time, bacon and cured or smoked sausage such as Spanish chorizo or French saucisson will survive happily, as will many a hard cheese. Eggs can be surprisingly resilient too, especially if you use the old trick of rolling them in melted butter before packing them away. Of all the ingredients you're likely to take, milk is probably the shortest lived. As a reliable substitute we carry cartons of UHT to take over when the fresh stuff runs out. For those who remember the foul taste of this suspect liquid in the past, it may come as a pleasant surprise to find that this ever-fresh milk doesn't even taste too bad.

Dehydrated beetroot-burger mix.

Then there are the inevitable packets of pasta, noodles and rice, and we often carry at least one bag of flour for simple baking.

Mind you, even with our tendency to start by cutting and frying an onion or two, or mixing up a bread mix from various labelled bags, we know that it is sometimes either going to be too hard, or just take too long, to prepare a meal from scratch. Cold and tired, with the lake or seashore already embraced by another long dark winter night, it is sometimes all too appealing to break open a tin or three of something that will soon be hot and filling, even if perhaps slightly bland. In amongst our bags of vegetables and flour you will always find quite a few tins of soup or sachets of something long-lasting and easy to cook.

Actually, we have another trick up our sleeves, courtesy of a Canadian food dehydrator made by a company called Excalibur. This machine not only dries all our surplus apples each autumn, but also allows us to fine tune the production of some excellent dried meals. You can even reduce meat dishes to a small, light and easy to carry package, although I must admit we haven't yet quite built up the courage to do so. Many a spicy vegetable broth or curry has travelled with us though, sometimes for months, before being tipped from an airtight plastic bag into a pan.

With the addition of water alone, what tastes almost as good as a fresh, homemade meal is available in a matter of minutes. It is good to know what's gone into the things you eat. You can also enjoy these meals dry as a snack. Soups for example, come out of the bag as slightly chewy crisps. I believe some people call this leather – a fairly apt name that hints at the texture, if not the taste.

Beyond the broad expanse of food choice, the following might be worth adding to your 'always carry' list:

- Cooking oil
- Salt and pepper
- Stock cubes
- Sugar
- Teabags and/or instant coffee, hot chocolate, etc.
- A few spices and dried herbs
- Water. This may seem strange, and fresh usable water is nearly always available, particularly if you carry a filter, but life is so much easier when first arriving at your chosen campsite if water is readily available to make a cup of tea straight away.

Luxuries, or semi-luxuries depending on the way you look at things, include:

- Ground coffee – and a stainless steel cafetière.
- A lemon – good with any fish that might be caught.

And while on the subject of fish, or anything else edible out there, it is great to add to your meal by gleaning, picking and angling, but unless you are very good at it, it is best not to rely on these additions to the pot. Pack food for the duration, and consider any 'findings' as a bonus.

Finally, if you are fairly new to all this camping lark, it is so much better to lug too much food around than too little.

Cutting tools – axes, saws and knives

Even if you have no intention of using a wood fire at your camp, I'd argue that each of these tools has a place in your kit, certainly the saw and knife. When it comes to providing emergency tent poles, spare tent pegs, a replacement cooking spatula, tarp supports or even a mast for a touch of canoe sailing, the saw will come in very handy, and none of these tasks could really be achieved without a knife. As soon as a wood fire is brought into play an axe can be very useful too.

Even as a fire user, if it came to advising a prospective camper between an axe and a saw, and assuming a good knife was carried, I would, slightly hesitantly, go for the saw. I suspect it is more useful, and potentially less dangerous in unskilled hands than the axe. And if wood of a sensible modest size is sourced and sawn, a knife can be used successfully for the final splitting. Saying all this, I would much rather take both. So what sort of axe?

The axe

My first comment will be to advise you to avoid anything on offer in a standard tool store. Look instead, either at the second-hand market or towards Sweden.

Most modern mass-produced offerings in the UK, and elsewhere in much of Europe are, to put it simply, crude, often too heavy and basically unpleasant to use. Fortunately, with a country still swathed in trees, Sweden has developed and maintained an enviable axe-making tradition. Their hand-forged products are quite simply beautiful to look at and a pleasure to use. Possibly because they are what I came across first, I favour the products of Gränsfors Bruks, but axes made by Hultafors are unlikely to let you down, and the Wetterlings output looks appealing too.

Mind you, Scandinavian axes aren't cheap, and this is where it's good to know that Britain used to boast a pretty good collection of makers too. If you can find something produced by one of the now defunct manufacturers such as Elwell, Brades or Gilpin, or even an elderly Spear and Jackson, you shouldn't be disappointed. These old British axes can sometimes be picked up in reasonable condition at car boot

The sort of thing you can pick up at a car boot sale. Cheap and tatty, this 'Kent' pattern hatchet will make a useful tool with a little care and attention.

An example of a hand-forged Scandinavian hatchet, this one made by Husqvarna.

A good axe – The Gränsfors Scandinavian Forest Axe.

sales for just a few pounds. Fairly shoddy-looking examples may set you back even less, and relatively little effort or time is usually needed to bring them back into working order. At worst, the outlay will be no more than the cost of a new handle.

And so to size …

My initial suggestion is simple. You don't need what is commonly referred to in North America and Britain as a felling axe. These job-specific tools (the hint is in the name) are too heavy in the head, and too long in the shaft for convenient camp use. Unless you are an experienced axe user, any felling or limb cutting is probably best approached with a bow saw. The only job for which an axe is infinitely better suited is splitting the sawn results.

For many, a small axe, often referred to as a hatchet, with a head weight of just under 0.5kg (1lb) and a handle length of around 35cm (13ins) will do. Easy to use single-handed, it can also be wielded with two hands as well – just.

For more controlled double-handed use, and usually still light enough for most people to manage with one hand, an axe with a handle of approximately 50cm (19ins) in length and head weight of around 0.75kg (1.5lb) offers a more versatile tool. An axe of this size, and the Gränsfors Bruks Small Forest Axe is a good example, allows other cutting tasks to be undertaken easily as confidence in handling grows.

There is also another advantage to an axe with a longer handle – it is invariably safer than one with a shorter version, the head of a wayward axe with a longer helve being more likely to hit the ground than you. This benefit becomes more pronounced if some of the safety measures suggested later, on page 145, are applied.

For the record, and as photographs show it, I use a Gränsfors Bruks Scandinavian Forest Axe. With a 65cm (25ins) handle, and a head weighing around 1kg (2lb), this is quite a big axe. Despite its size though, and an ability to manage smaller scale felling with ease, it is still light and small enough for me to use with one hand when the situation demands.

Oh, and a final comment. Any good axe maker will provide this tool with a leather cover (sheath) to clip over the head. An essential item, to protect you, your belongings, and the blade.

Saws

Saws also come in all shapes and sizes, with many putting up a good performance. I've even heard of people taking the standard carpenters' saw into the wild with success. Folding or collapsible saws are available, usually with a wooden frame. These are often perfectly serviceable, but I've always felt that the carrying capacity of your canoe means that you can avoid the need to use a saw that has to be taken apart and then rebuilt again with each move of camp. Given the storage space, I suggest you turn your thoughts to a bow saw.

These days, bow saws usually come in one of three blade lengths – 52.5cm (21ins), 60cm (24ins) or 75.9cm (30ins) – with the shortest often held in a triangular frame. Although the large and small saw will do, I definitely prefer the 60cm (24ins) version, which is big enough for almost all jobs, and easy to handle. Saws should always come with a plastic clip-on blade guard, and in my book, the best are made in, you've guessed it, Sweden.

In addition to a bow saw I also carry a small folding pruning saw. This isn't essential, but stored in my personal bag, it tends to travel with me at nearly all times, and often comes in handy.

The knife

And the best camping knives come from … ?

Well, yes the Swedes do make some very good knives, but then so do the Finns, and (a little flag waving here) the British too.

But before moving on to discuss the main event – the fixed blade knife – I do want to mention two other knives that travel everywhere with me.

A bow saw can be just as useful as an axe, possibly more so.

My small folding pruning saw.

An Opinel.

An inexpensive knife from Finland. Even with only a short blade, this will manage most jobs.

That first implement, mentioned already, is the Swiss Army knife. This is more a multi-purpose tool than just a cutting blade, and always to be found somewhere amongst my kit. As is another knife, this time from the other end of the technological spectrum, the French Opinel. This masterpiece of design, still produced by the Opinel family, is a star. It is simple, cheap, efficient, and, because it folds, is small enough to store easily. It can also be locked open, saving fingers, and turning it into something almost as useful as a fixed blade tool. Ignore the more modern stainless steel (Inox) versions, and a perfectly decent carbon steel (Carbone) blade is yours. This blade is also quite thin, making the Opinel a great emergency kitchen knife. The fine blade also complements the stronger and broader version on my fixed knife. Produced in a range of numbered sizes, I've always chosen a no. 8. If memory serves right, I may have used pocket money to buy my first, in Brittany, when I was about nine (and a half). We were required to carry a knife at school then. How the world has changed.

And as I've mentioned carbon steel, I will run with the subject for a moment. Although admittedly prone to oxidation if not looked after properly, the cutting edge and easy sharpening qualities of a good carbon steel blade far outweigh, at least in my book, the alleged benefits of stainless steel. When I buy a knife I want a versatile blade, ideally found in differentially tempered and hardened steel, which works with me on a wide range of cutting tasks.

For my main cutting tool, the blade needs to possess that very tricky balance of being fine enough for delicate work, yet sufficiently robust to take some reasonable battering (such as in wood-splitting work). It has to be easy to sharpen, and attached very firmly to a comfortable handle. I want it to come with a sheath from which it can be extracted easily, but isn't going to fall. Oh, and it is best if it also looks good too. Tall order? Yes, and the reason why a good knife can cost so much.

Not that you have to pay through the teeth, and I suggest a look at some of the Finnish knives if you are after value for money.

If you are willing to pay a little though, it is worth doing some homework and reading reviews. Some very good knives are being made out there, and the bushcraft world tends to know about them. Prices vary from bearable to scary, but remember that a good knife will be one of the most important canoe camping tools after your paddle – and actually, if you break that, a good axe and knife can soon be pressed into action to make a serviceable replacement.

Knife blade length is tricky, and I would suggest choosing something with as short a blade as will perform the tasks you have in mind. I always carry an axe, so hardly ever need to split wood with my knife. For this reason I tend to manage perfectly well with a blade of only 8cm (3ins). If you do see yourself splitting wood with your knife, then something in the 10 to 13cm (4 to 5ins) range will be better.

And a last comment about all cutting tools, particularly if, like me, you intend to paddle on the sea. Just remember to rub a little oil onto the metal parts every now and again. A slight chore, but much better than rusty blades.

Serenity.

Clothing – from footwear to hats

For experienced outdoor types there is little I'm likely to be able to offer here. If you've been out there paddling about for long, the chances are that you fine-tuned your boat clothing successfully years ago. For those still in the fascinating process of getting it right I'm going to be rather annoying by suggesting that trial and error is likely to be the best approach. The problem is that what one paddler considers the bee's knees in clothing, the next cheery canoeist will think best dropped on the nearest campfire.

Much of the problem is down to the bewildering range of choice, with canoeing kit manufactured from a staggering variety of efficient and hardwearing synthetic materials. There is then an almost equally large assortment of traditional wool and cotton garb. The options are almost endless.

A good Gore-Tex coat (and trousers) in between showers in typical Scottish winter weather.

All that said, and already feeling rather guilty at the thought that I may be failing in my duties, here are a few considerations, in truth no more than my own preferences. Please note though that these choices suit me, and may not impress you at all if you try them.

Modern fabrics are wonderful at almost all times while canoe camping – that is until you find yourself too close to a naked flame, an inevitable element of a wood fire. While cotton or wool might singe a little, usually warning you of impending disaster well in advance by producing a foul stink, oil-based fabrics just melt – fast. They also have a tendency to sometimes catch fire. Nasty.

I must admit to struggling a little with this one. Much as I love to keep dry inside something incorporating a Gore-Tex or eVent layer, I've grown pretty bored of find-ing holes in these expensive garments, caused by stray sparks – a distinct drawback of open fire usage. These days I tend to try to manage with cotton outer layers that the manufacturers claim to be almost waterproof. They're not bad, but in the end, unless you use something that doesn't breathe at all, and this really isn't a good idea, nothing keeps the rain out as well as a garment fitted with one of the modern breathable membranes.

While mentioning cotton, it is here that I feel the need to raise two other personal prejudices, one negative the other more upbeat.

Perhaps I should start with the particular clothing department in which I have ban-ished cotton almost for good from my holdall. This involves base layers, or what we used to call underwear. Unless it is a baking hot day, when I may be tempted into a cotton T-shirt, I studiously avoid these cold clammy items. Not that I am any happier with the latest, high-wicking synthetic sensation either; smelly things that just fill the sea with yet more indestructible and damaging yarn filaments. No, my outdoor world was transformed one day in a Katmandu store when a cheery young New Zealander persuaded me to try merino. I now rarely leave home inside anything else, although other brands such as Icebreaker and Smartwool have since entered the mix.

Another hole in a man-made fabric resulting from a stray fire spark.

There's that Tilley hat again – this time in central Sweden.

Now in support of cotton I must raise what I feel to be the thorny issue of Tilley hats. If any single garment is guilty of having become something of a canoe clothing cliché it is this almost ubiquitous head covering. Spot a canoe in the distance, and eight times out of ten the approaching paddler will be sporting one. The problem is, so will I. The thing is, they work, brilliantly. So much for individuality.

At most times of the year canoeing can be undertaken in whatever clothing you might normally choose to wear out camping. Waterproof stuff in wet weather, cool stuff in the summer (at least over a rare sunny day or two) and warmer stuff when it grows chilly. Cold weather does demand a little more thought though, even extending as far as considering the use of a drysuit or other dedicated paddling garments (with the whole matter considered in detail on page 195).

Beyond these specialist garments, clothing collections will inevitably vary quite a bit. Differences can depend on personal taste, the time of year, intended campsite location and expected weather. The following lists, which don't include purely canoeing gear, are therefore offered more as a form of potential checklist than anything else. You may well not need, or want, to take everything suggested, but these items might at least be worth considering.

Warm weather canoe camping

Susannah's idea of warm weather camping clothes.

- Sunhat (a good tough one, and Tilley products are pretty robust, and can keep all but the worst rain off too).
- At least one spare shirt or T-shirt (a replacement covers any accidents, if nothing else).
- At least one spare pair of trousers.
- Shorts.
- At least one spare set of underwear.
- At least one additional pair of socks.
- Sandals for warm evenings around the campsite (dedicated watersport versions can be worn all day).
- A thinnish jumper, mid-weight fleece or similar for cold evenings.
- A lightweight waterproof coat with a hood (in whatever material you prefer).
- Lightweight waterproof trousers.

You may also wish to take swimming gear (and a towel). I'll also mention toiletries here, just so that they aren't forgotten.

These days I seem to wear a Buff around my neck at almost all times. These clever tubular things provide protection from sun or wind, and, of course, offer almost all the other potential benefits the makers suggest in their advertising.

Cold weather canoe camping

In addition to the list above, during the colder months you may well wish to take:

- A warm hat (wool or synthetic).
- A scarf, or, to my mind, much better a 'Polar' Buff, or similar.
- Warm socks (and spares).
- Gloves. Often a good idea to have a thin inner pair, perhaps in a modern wind-blocking fabric, with an insulated waterproof pair to go over the top. I prefer waterproof overmitts.
- A warm wool jumper, a thick fleece or a modern insulated jacket/smock (the last preferably not down-filled unless sporting a waterproof shell). You would probably do best to choose something with some form of synthetic insulation such as Primaloft. These retain much of their warmth retaining qualities when wet. Wool also has the advantage of being an effective insulator, even when soaked.
- Thermal leggings.

Sensible cold weather clothing.

To cover accidental soakings, as well as giving another chance to wear something clean, at least one spare outfit should also be packed elsewhere amongst your kit.

Footwear

Many people appear to manage perfectly well through most of the year in some form of robust laced boot. This all seems fine to me until you meet the water's edge, which doesn't take long of course when canoe camping. I then spend much of the experience with wet feet.

To counteract this problem (well, I see it as a problem) I turn to a pair of sandals in warm weather, preferably ones designed for watersport use. Something that can be worn all day, in or out of the water, suits me, and they soon dry off.

Sandals in summer.

Of course in Britain, there all too soon comes the time when sandals just don't offer enough protection. At these colder times of year, and keen to be able to wade around my canoe, hopping in and out at will without fear of wet feet, I am more than happy to wear wellingtons, despite the dire warnings from some quarters. Even having read, and often heard, all the arguments against wellies, I just can't see how a pair will pull you under if you go in – many pairs of rubber boots even float! I do acknowledge that a cheap workman's pair, with a gaping mouth, may well hinder progress if forced to swim, and these are worth avoiding. Even when camping in summer, in areas plagued by biting insects, I am happy to don my wellies, despite the risk that my feet might grow a little hot and bothered.

As a very good compromise, I have started to experiment with thin rubber yachting boots. Light, and close fitting at the top, these can be long enough for most wading around a canoe. And I don't see dinghy or yacht sailors worrying much about swimming in them.

Wellies when the weather is cooler.

Torches and lamps

Our candle lantern.

Rarely has a single piece of kit had such an impact on my enjoyment of camping as the headtorch. Over the years I've used a myriad of standard hand-held torches, Tilley lamps, old-fashioned hurricane lamps and candle lamps. On one bizarre occasion I even employed a flaming torch on a stick, the sort you usually only see in old Frankenstein movies. While I have retained a soft spot for the candle lantern for use in a tent, the rest have long ago been abandoned.

Bright, long-lasting, and crucially, leaving both hands free, the headtorch is a permanent campsite feature each evening. If it isn't in place and in use, it will be hung around my neck in readiness. Sometimes it will remain there well into the next day, and family members like to guess when I'll finally notice it's still there.

A torch, along with a good whistle, can also provide a very valuable role as pieces of safety kit. For comments on signalling for help see page 208.

In the tent the candle lanterns are accompanied by a wind-up lamp. This produces a rather cold dead light, but at least nothing runs out, or nothing that a little frantic handle turning can't deal with.

Making good use of a headtorch.

Repair kit

If you're lucky you may never need this. As you will probably experience all the inevitable mishaps and calamities that accompany a trip into the wild, this bag of goodies may well prove to be one of your most useful piece of kit, or at least one you'll be very grateful you packed.

Of course if you were to include something to cover every eventuality you'd probably never push off from the shore. The trick is in identifying things that can be shoehorned into offering a range of repair opportunities (a useful strategy when choosing any piece of camping kit). I start with a stout canvas or modern dry bag, into which I put:

- Duct tape. This smallish roll of super sticky material has wangled me out of more potential scrapes than just about any other single item. It can be expensive, or at least seem so until you need it badly, and it is worth buying the best you can find. Agricultural merchants often sell decent stuff at a reasonable price. Actually, agricultural merchants sell lots of very useful things at sensible prices. Farmers know what they want, and don't care to pay over the odds. This tape will mend just about anything, and if enough layers or turns are used, the repair can be unexpectedly strong. When hill or mountain walking I wind a few turns around my ice axe or walking pole shaft. It's surprising how often it comes in handy.

- Plastic pull ties. These are almost as useful as duct tape, and I often use them in combination – a sort of pull tie/duct tape composite. Almost any size and length will come in handy one day.

- Wire. Random lengths of anything you can bend easily, and which keeps its shape, have so many uses. That green, plastic-coated garden stuff is good, but my favourite is lightweight fencing wire. If you also carry a pair of pliers to twist the ends together, a very tight binding can be produced, holding things together where duct tape and plastic pull ties aren't really up to the job.

- Pliers. Particularly useful when that tight, twisted wire repair is needed, but offering a host of other mend or make benefits. Other tools may also be welcome, but pliers are where to start. While a basic pair is fine, some of the multi-tools, such as the Leatherman or Gerber, offer decent pliers, and a range of other useful items as well.

- Araldite (or a similar glue) – for more delicate jobs where a strong glue is helpful.

- A specialist repair kit for your self-inflating sleeping mat, assuming you're using one of course.

- String – should be self-explanatory.

- Needle and thread – a few biggish needles and some stout thread never go amiss. And while on this subject, why is it that only the more expensive pieces of clothing ever seem to get ripped?

My repair kit – and an interesting test, as this shows what I discovered without pre-preparing the contents. An assortment of pull ties and wire, a couple of lengths of string, two rolls of duct tape (and one of insulating tape), Araldite, various strengths of cotton thread and two needles (one a touch large, the other a little too small), a candle stub (to wax threads), a pair of pliers, a Swiss Army card (very handy, and I'd wondered where it was), three Jubilee clips, two hefty bolts (with nuts and washers), and spare sections of rubber inner tube and canvas – oh, and a whetstone. Should manage most things.

Safety kit

Risk, and how you might reduce it while canoe camping, is considered on pages 189 (on the water) and 202 (on land) below. Here though are some thoughts on what to take in order to help, either in reducing the chance that unpleasant things will happen, or helping to deal with the results if you are unlucky enough to still have things go wrong.

First aid kit

Pre-packed first aid kits are available from a whole range of sources. Many are designed to cater for a specified number of people, and it makes obvious sense to carry one that covers everyone in the party. Kits designed for mountain use are a good start, but I think they are still a little light on the bulkier and often most useful items such as wound dressings and bandages. As we aren't constrained by

A few useful items spilling from a comprehensive first aid kit – this time in a surprising green dry bag.

A decent compass.

A selection of good maps – Ordnance Survey 1:50,000 or 1:25,000 sheets (and a useful dry bag) and Harvey 1:40,000 map, which is waterproof, so it doesn't need one.

the same weight and size limits as our pedestrian explorer cousins, it makes sense to top up.

I also like to have a good eyewash and eyebath. Sensitive things eyes, and these two additions can make so much difference should something nasty happen.

May I also suggest you take cling film. This proposal shouldn't surprise a first aider, but for those wondering if I've lost it a bit here, this food covering makes a very useful substitute skin should you be unfortunate enough to burn your home grown version. More on this later (page 204).

Add to all this more antiseptic, a good antihistamine cream (possibly some antihistamine tablets as well), and a packet of standard paracetamol and/or aspirin painkillers, and you are close to being able to deal with most unpleasant eventualities.

Map and compass

As simple as that. Just ensure that each is appropriate for the job.

Any half-decent compass will show you where north is of course. Better though to put your hands on either one of the dedicated models with a clear plastic baseplate of the sort made by companies such as Silva, or one capable of taking a sight bearing.

Maps come in all shapes and sizes. At the risk of upsetting other map makers out there, I would stick, in Britain at least, to ones made either by the Ordnance Survey (or OS for short) or Harvey. As this section covers only what to take, and not what to do with them, I will add only that OS map sheets with a scale of 1:50,000 or 1:25,000, or Harvey maps with a scale of 1:40,000 are best suited to your purpose.

Some OS maps come laminated, and a number of the Harvey range are printed directly onto a plastic sheet, making both types the preferred map for wet weather use – another way of describing the outdoors in Britain.

If you can only put your hands on a traditional paper map, it is worth purchasing a waterproof map case. Some, such as those made by Ortlieb for example, come with soft, rubbery see-through covers that don't take your eye out when being thrown about by the wind – or the British outside again.

All European countries have their own OS equivalent or equivalents.

The Acme Thunderer.

A whistle

The louder the better, and if you expect to spend much time next to the sea, with all that salty water, probably best made of plastic. Call me an old fogey, but I still have a soft spot for the Acme Thunderer. Advice on how your whistle can come in handy when in an emergency can be found on page 208.

A knife

Discussed already of course, but mentioned again as it is such an important safety item. Anyone working on the water with ropes, and that includes canoeists (painter, throw bag lines, fishing lines, etc.) should carry a knife for safety reasons alone. Finding yourself in the unfortunate position of being hooked up to something that wants to pull you into or under water is bad. Not having a knife immediately to hand in these situations, and that really means in a sheath attached to a belt or PFD strapping, doesn't bear thinking about. And this is just the most obvious safety benefit on offer.

Sunglasses and sunblock

OK, so this now runs the real risk of being patronising – it's just that I'm very good at heading out onto the water without either. You would think that a few five or ten mile journeys, heading straight into a low sun, would have taught me a lesson by now. Well it has – to nag you into not making the same mistake.

Our slightly scruffy throw bag.

A good generous bailer, with a handy sponge wedged in place.

Boat stuff

Carrying most of this kit should be second nature to an experienced paddler.

Individual buoyancy aids, or as they're currently called, personal floatation devices (PFDs) are a must, and these are much improved if they actually fit the person expected to wear them. Purchasing PFDs from a good paddlesport shop, where sensible advice can be sought on fit and suitability for the task in mind, is a very good idea.

Throw bags are also a sensible addition. These are effectively a floating rope in a bag, designed to allow the user to chuck a lifeline to someone in difficulty on or in the water.

We take a spare paddle – usually one each. This may seem slight overkill, and I'd have to agree that two are unlikely to break on the same trip. My concern is getting at the sole spare when you need it. As it will be stowed close to me at the stern, I'll have no problem grabbing it should my first choice snap or go over the side. But what about Susannah in the bow? In normal circumstances, it would be relatively easy to turn and ask me to pull it free and pass it forward. But what of the more extreme conditions of wind, tide or underwater obstruction, in fact those circumstances most likely to result in a breakage or loss in the first place? Not so simple then I suspect, and a good reason to have a spare bow paddle somewhere up front too.

A good bailer. I take a bucket, as it has so many other uses around a campsite. A generous brick-shaped block of sponge goes in here. This is very useful for removing those last few pints of water from the bottom of the canoe. I deliberately choose a piece that is longer than the diameter of my bucket base so that it wedges there in place – or should.

For most trips I also like to have a length of good quality rope, perhaps somewhere between 10 and 20m long. Old climbing rope is excellent, coiling and knotting well, although sometime it is a little too stretchy. If you can afford it, good soft braided line almost always pays for itself sooner or later. As I often carry a small anchor (at sea anyway), a length of rope is already stored with this. And speaking of anchors – they're not so important on most occasions, but one of those wee umbrella-types can be very useful to the keen canoe fisher.

The other day someone asked me if I carried flares. I don't, but having given this some thought, can think of no reason why this wouldn't be a good idea, especially when travelling on the coast. Here, a VHF radio might also be a good idea. We don't carry one, partly due to cost – although the price may seem much more reasonable when you need it. I understand that proper training and a licence should

A PFD in use in Switzerland. It's even colour coordinated.

A bothy bag.

accompany its use. We tend to rely on two mobile phones, charged up and stored somewhere waterproof. All very well, until the signal goes of course.

I do carry a small radio, not to keep track of global events or the result of the latest test match (actually I may occasionally check the score), but for the shipping forecast, or at least the latest weather predictions. Knowing that the next couple of days will be calm and dry is reassuring. Being warned of an impending gale could avoid all sorts of unpleasantness.

The observant may have spotted that I haven't mentioned additional buoyancy for the canoe. While I see this as very sensible addition for non-camping canoeing, I am happy to rely on my packed kit to provide this important service when heading out to put up a tent. More on this subject on page 104.

Land stuff

If travelling in cold weather, and despite having a tent with you, a bothy bag makes a very sensible addition to your safety kit. These lightweight emergency shelters pack down small, so are very easy to carry. Should someone get wet, injured and/or very cold then these temporary structures can provide a very helpful heat trap and wind barrier. Using bothy bags is discussed further on page 198. Choose one in a bright colour and you also have something for a helicopter or lifeboat to look out for in the unhappy situation in which you have had to put out a call for help.

Although water from a stream in the highlands of Scotland is probably safe to drink, and you can always boil it to be sure, it may be useful to add some form of filtration system to your kit for those times when a fire or stove either isn't available or practical. For this job we carry a small blue Katadyn filter. A touch slow in action, but it seems to do the trick.

As they say on television – other brands are available. The Steripen system looks interesting, but I haven't yet tried it. I have used water purification tablets, but thankfully not for a long time, and not since I owned a reliable filter.

One last suggestion – antibacterial hand wash. This may seem a bit namby pamby, but I'm sure a quick hand rub with this bug-killing stuff before cooking or eating has nipped a few potential cases of gut rot in the bud before now. Why risk wasting limited canoe camping time feeling unwell?

Insect repellent

Health and safety? Unfortunately, yes.

A selection of insect repellents.

It's true that much of the benefit from a good insect repellent comes from the enhanced ability to enjoy the whole canoe camping experience uninterrupted. Remember, you will be by water all day and all night. Keeping buzzy bitey things at arm's length can make a big difference, whether they are the infamous west coast Scottish midge (yes, they are that bad), or the almost as irritating Swedish mosquito.

Sadly, there are a couple of more serious reasons to keep certain insects at bay (or out in the bay). Lyme disease is carried by seemingly ever greater numbers of deer ticks, and is relatively common in Scotland. Tick-borne encephalitis lurks in Scandinavia. Worryingly it may even have reached UK shores. Lyme disease can be really quite unpleasant, especially if left untreated. In rare cases Tick-borne encephalitis can kill. I will address this whole issue further on page 206, but for the kit list all I can say is add an effective repellent to your stores, and consider buying a dedicated tick remover. I use one provided by the vet for use on my mother's retriever.

Consider taking a head net. Here in northern Sweden we were glad we had ours.

For those who have a real problem with small biting monsters, consider taking a head net. I once thought people who wore these were soft shandy-drinking southerners, until I tried to strap my canoe to the roof of the van at the upper end of Loch Etive one summer evening. I bought one the next day.

All those things that you forget

Perhaps it would be fairer to say all the things that I forget. One way round this predicament, for me at least, is to try and store all these odds and ends in a single bag, and then try to remember to take that. This bulging canvas shoulder bag is clipped to the stern thwart with a karabiner. In this, and in addition to all the things already mentioned (duplicating many), will go:

A good load – that should include everything.

- A sun hat or beanie hat depending what's already on my head

- Sunglasses (even in winter these can sometimes be welcome)

- Matches – in a dry bag, with

- Tinder (usually birch bark)

- A fire steel

- My headtorch

- Tiny radio

- Spare AAA batteries (for the headtorch and radio)

- Binoculars (small and gas-filled)

- A spork

- An A5 waterproof Ortlieb map case

- A map of the area visited

- A Silva compass

- A whistle

- A Swiss Army knife

- Opinel knife

- A folding wood saw

- A silver propelling pencil (I'm told standard wooden pencils do a perfectly good job)

- A notebook (no, I'm not that organised, and rarely write anything in it)

- A file to take any nasty nicks out of the axe blade

- A small whetstone to finish this job

- Spare boot laces (which have many other uses than just holding your boots on)

- A tide timetable (sometimes even for the area I'm paddling in)

- Paracetamol tablets

- Antihistamine cream

- And finally, but very importantly, a Sigg bottle of drinking water

And yes, the bag is quite big, but still sometimes hard to shut.

My bag - and not looking too tightly packed either.

Sensible additions

While in no way essential to canoe camping success, there are a few more kit additions worth considering – although I note that the list I've produced does bear an uncanny parallel to my own interests.

Fishing rods

Perhaps what I am trying to encourage here is recognition that a canoe, due to its carrying capacity, can support a number of activities out there in the wilds.

Now it has to be admitted that I am a pretty keen fisherman, but with all that water close to your campsite, the addition of a rod or two and a bag of tackle provides not only a diverting, possibly even fun activity, but the chance to add to your meals.

Rods are best protected by some form of tube. This can be as cheap and cheery as a length of plastic pipe with a cap at each end (examples leaning against the van at the end of the chapter). This and a tackle bag aren't going to take up much room.

In England and Wales, if you wish to fish on a river or lake, you'll need a rod licence to accompany any permission from the owner.

Cameras

Yes, it's true, I also like to take photographs, sometimes rather a lot, but memories do fade, and good results can be produced these days by even the smallest digital compacts. Without costing the earth, some are even waterproof. There really is no reason that I can think of to not take a camera – other than wishing to avoid modern trappings of course.

Binoculars

These aren't just useful for watching seals, otters, dunlin, deer, eagles and the rest, but also offer a chance to spy out a potential campsite in a distant bay, or decide whether the one you know about is already occupied without having to make a lake crossing to find out. I also find them useful in spotting navigation hazards.

Better binoculars are gas-filled to help keep the damp out.

Boots and rucksacks

And anything else that allows you to walk, clamber or climb near your campsite.

If you are planning to wander away from the shore though, and there isn't a member of the party willing to babysit, then you will also need to consider kit security. I can't think of anything to protect a campsite, and suspect that any blind faith in human good nature won't be enough.

When all the camping kit is packed, then some rather useful wire mesh bags can be bought. Even the largest aren't that big though and they are pricey.

Ready for the off.

To secure canoes, the best tactic I've found is to use the long lengths of plastic-covered wire, with a hard plastic ball at one end and a loop at the other, used by surfers to safeguard their boards on top of a car or van. Hints regarding use, and other tactics are provided on page 176.

Who to take

This section may seem an odd addition. In many ways it is. As someone writing a book intended to encourage people to head out into the wild with a tent and canoe, it shouldn't come as a surprise that I'd like to see anyone willing to take part given that opportunity. It is included though to encourage all those contemplating the prospect to take a moment to consider whether they are ready for the experience.

Things can go wrong on land of course, and I could make a very boring list of the potential problems that might be faced by an unfortunate camper. Serious as some of these are, they probably diminish quite a bit in comparison with the sort of thing that could go wrong on the water.

Now this is where I find myself in a bit of a dilemma. As a strong believer that one of the definitions of a mature and sensible society is its ability to let an adult feel free to take risks and to find out for themselves where their limits are, I am keen to ensure that any comment I make is a call for consideration not prohibition. I think it was T.S. Elliot who once wrote, "Only those who will risk going too far can possibly find out how far one can go". All I suggest is that you take just a moment to decide whether you really have the boat experience – canoe control, weather, tide and current awareness and the rest – needed to bring those risks within reasonable parameters (whatever they are). Until familiarity is developed, a canoe can be a frustratingly difficult vessel to handle. Do you really want to be out there on the water, struggling to deal with basic management, when something decides to go wrong?

Maybe you do of course. The question is then, do you want the possibility of putting anyone else to the trouble, or risk, of coming to your assistance?

My other intention in this brief section is to urge those planning for the off to give some thought to those they are taking with them. This includes friends and colleagues, who may, or may not, prove to be an unreasonable responsibility should things turn a little awry. Some people display all their best characteristics when things go wrong, others very much their worst. It is rarely fun to find out that your canoe camping pal falls into the second category as the wind picks up and the bow paddle breaks at the very moment a trawler is spotted bearing down, seemingly oblivious of your existence.

And then there are children.

Now while I am perfectly happy to see a not necessarily very experienced adult make an informed decision to give it a go, setting out for an adventure knowing that they may be pushing it a bit, this relaxed response evaporates instantly as soon as children are brought into the mix. In brief, if you are considering taking anyone under sixteen out onto the water, it must only be done by those completely confident in their all-round competence.

Adults have, or should have, the choice to do something daft every now and again. In my opinion children should also be availed of risk, but only carefully managed versions of peril and jeopardy, that seem pretty big to them, while in reality hardly existing at all.

The first day of the year – starting as we mean to carry on.

What To Take It All In - The Canoe

Choosing your canoe

Of course in any canoe camping mix, the key element must inevitably be the canoe. So what does a good camping canoe look like?

Well the easy answer, and one with considerable validity, is almost any canoe you manage to cast your eyes on. Assuming it was manufactured by someone reputable, just about any will do the trick. These are, after all, craft that have evolved through generations of use to carry loads efficiently and easily from one watery place to another. Some designs will inevitably accomplish the job better than others of course. So what about the perfect camping canoe?

Now that is tricky. Gather half a dozen experienced canoeists together and they will work their way around that one for days, and still probably not agree completely on an answer. The reason for this is that not all canoe camping expeditions are the same – one of their joys. You may wish to set out on your own for just one night, or two of you may envisage spending a week or more in exploration and tent pitching. Your chosen route may lie along a well-protected lake, mere or loch, perhaps a section of the Norfolk Broads for example, or you may have your sights set on a paddle along a fairly wild river or a section of partially exposed coast. Each choice has a bearing on the ideal vessel to support your expedition.

The parts of the canoe, or at least those mentioned in this book.

When considering something quite as beautiful as a canoe, it seems almost a shame to start analysing technical details, reducing this lovely vessel, even in discussion, into its constituent parts. But in order to assess what makes a particularly good camping canoe, the key elements need to be identified.

These can be broken down usefully into the following categories:

- Material
- Weight
- Length
- Width
- Cross-sectional hull profile
- Longitudinal hull profile
- Above waterline profile

See, I did warn that all this scrutiny does rather take the romance out of these fine vessels.

Materials

As this is intended as a realistic guide to canoe camping I will touch only briefly on wooden vessels. And before the howls of criticism rise from various watery spots, I hasten to add that this is not because I consider them inappropriate for the job, very far from it. Given the chance, a cedar and canvas canoe, for example, makes an absolutely ideal support for anyone wishing to head into the wild with a tent. Even birch bark models are far tougher than most people imagine, and if ever damaged, easily repaired if you know how. After all, they would hardly have ended up as such a universally employed craft for so long if they couldn't fit this role.

The problem lies in the initial outlay. I recognise that few prospective canoe campers are going to be able to part with the sometimes very serious amounts of cash needed to become an owner of one of these floating gems. For those that can, please consider a wooden canoe for the job. The return will almost certainly outweigh the expense in so many ways. You might even be able to build one yourself.

For the rest of us, there is still a wide range of choice.

Although most canoes on the market will be available in one form of plastic or another, or at least something that to a non-scientist looks and feels like plastic, aluminium models can be found. In summary, these are tough, rigid, largely maintenance free, and sometimes pretty noisy. Every knock will be heard. Hit hard and they will also split, but then so will most canoes.

A 16 foot cedar and canvas canoe built by Alex Comb of Stewart River Boatworks. A great camping support vessel.

A very pretty birch bark canoe, built in the 1880s, and now in the care of the Royal Albert Memorial Museum, Exeter.

Left: a polyethylene (Mad River Explorer, on the left) and Royalex (Wenonah Prospector) at rest after providing sterling camping support.

Right: an aluminium canoe, built by Grumman, and part of the West Cumbria Canoe Club fleet.

This is certainly the case with some of the fancy fibreglass, graphite or Kevlar composites out there. Of course, what they lack in relative robustness is more than made up for in weight, or lack of it. For anyone looking for a canoe that is easy to carry, then a Kevlar or graphite blend hull is the choice for you, if you can afford it. They may be light to portage, but these lovely craft are heavy on the pocket.

At the other end of the cost spectrum comes polypropylene and polyethylene. Don't be put off by the cheap(ish) price. Purchase of a polywhatever canoe may not hit the bank balance very hard, but you can still find some very competent and almost maintenance free vessels in this material. They may not possess the rigidity of canoes in more expensive composite blends, and they may weigh a few pounds more, but anyone on a tight budget shouldn't be put off.

A splendid compromise when it comes to canoe materials arrives in the form of Royalex, a plastic sandwich or laminate that is strong and yet reasonably light. It is tough, shrugs off most impacts, and almost bounces back into shape following knocks that would cripple many other craft. It even has a foam core to help canoe buoyancy – a very useful characteristic should things go awry. The only problem is that as I edit this section, rumours that the manufacture of this extremely popular canoe material might cease have been confirmed. The latest news is that an American canoe manufacturer may have a suitable replacement in the wings. I'm sure many wilderness canoeists will be hoping this is true.

Left: a fine canoeing tradition – the 'swap' – with me (left) trying a 15 foot British-built Kevlar boat. Light, stiff and capable.

Right: a Royalex canoe – our canoe, a 16 foot Prospector, made by Wenonah.

And should you still hanker for a wooden canoe, but a quick glance at your bank balance tells you that this dream may yet have to wait for a few more years, many models come with wooden gunwales as a optional extra, at a slight cost of course. To my perhaps slightly traditionalist eyes, those thin strips of ash or cherry can make quite a difference. Just remember to keep oiling them.

Weight

Actually, it would be dishonest to state that those few extra pounds found in some boats don't matter. It's surprising how just a couple can really make themselves felt when carrying your cherished craft. I hold a view that any pound over seventy has about twice the mass of any under that mysterious weight. Rubbish of course, but it can certainly feel like that as the centre thwart starts to dig into your shoulders. As a basic guide – under 60lb (27.2kg) is very good, over 70lb (31.8kg) isn't so hot. Some composite boats can weigh less than 50lb (22.7kg), and of course canoe dimensions play a big part here.

Length

Although historically canoes have been built in lengths of anything between 10 and over 40 ft (3 to 12m), you are unlikely to find many on the market measuring less than 13 or 14ft (4m) or more than 20ft (6m). Deciding on what will best serve your needs, the choice can fall anywhere between these two extremes, with that last word used intentionally.

By some strange quirk of canoe/human ratios a canoe of 16ft (4.9m) in length seems to provide something of an almost universal solution. As a rough rule of thumb, a solo paddler is unlikely to be served well by anything over this length. Rules are there for breaking of course, and some very impressive load carriers are available for the solo paddler at lengths quite a way beyond this. These are usually designed to allow lone travellers to carry sometimes quite considerable loads over long distances. In more usual situations someone on their own is likely to find a 15 or 16ft canoe fits the bill for almost all occasions.

When it comes to tandem travelling, a 16ft (4.9m) canoe again marks a useful starting length, and for many an end to their search. 15ft (4.6m) boats will do of course, with obvious limitations to carrying capacity. Canoes of 17ft (5.2m) or 18ft (5.5m) increase the load that can be taken, and often the ease of paddling too. By a quirk of physics, a longer canoe usually moves more easily through the water, and is almost invariably easier to keep in a straight line. Put simply, a longer canoe will carry more, but at the same time also weigh more and be that little bit more difficult to transport, either when portaged, or on the roof of a vehicle.

Width

It might be imagined that variations in canoe width, or beam, would be linked closely to the length. Interestingly, this seems to be the case only to a limited degree, and the width of a useable canoe remains almost constant between about 32 and 36ins (81 to 91cm). While length can be very much a matter of taste, you will probably do well to choose your craft with a beam between these measurements.

Anything much narrower, and while your canoe will be fast, carrying capacity is bound to be compromised, and stability will also suffer. Much more width will offer more room for kit, but at the expense of ease of paddling. Stability may not improve that much either, having much to do with cross-sectional profiles.

Hull profile – cross-section

For experienced canoeists, the next comment will not come as much of a surprise, but those new to these lovely craft are often baffled to find that a canoe with a flat bottom doesn't necessarily represent the best option when looking for stability.

Admittedly, in flat calm conditions, a canoe with a flat base will feel remarkably solid and steady. And paddled across a smooth lake on a still and beautiful autumn day everything will feel very dependable.

Problems arise as soon as the water you're floating on starts to move up and down, and if it is planned to explore anywhere even slightly wild, particularly on larger lakes or the sea, this soon happens. Waves are a certainty.

Where a canoe has a more rounded profile the movement of water around the hull has, to put it simply, little to grab hold of. Conversely, a flatter base inevitably requires a fairly sharp turn to meet the sides. This angle offers the wave something to grasp, inevitably resulting in a wobble. Matters are made worse, sometimes quite a lot worse, as the canoe tips beyond a certain point. A canoe with a rounded profile has much the same amount of hull in the water at whatever angle it leans. This means that it retains its stability. Tipped on its side, a flat-bottomed canoe literally ends up balanced on a corner, with much less hull in the water. The results can be a little unnerving.

 Mind you, a hull with a completely arched or rounded cross-section would feel too wobbly. Fortunately a compromise is available in what is called a shallow arched profile (see the photo of our upturned Prospector in the 'Materials' section above). Although V-shaped hulls are also popular (as found on the polyethylene Explorer in the same image), to my mind the shallow arch offers the perfect solution, resulting in a relatively fast craft with perhaps a slightly wobbly feel in general use until you are used to it, but with an inbuilt tendency to firm up on the lean, just when you need it.

Hull profile – longitudinal

And so to the next, and even more hotly debated, profile consideration, the shape of the hull from one end of your canoe to the other. Central to this discussion is what is called 'rocker'. Fortunately, even if hard to conclude, this matter is relatively easy to explain if I ask you to picture a canoe sat on flat, level ground. Imagine that you are viewing it from the side.

At one end of the spectrum you will find a few canoes where the two upright, or nearly upright ends, come almost right down to the ground, and the hull lies flat on the surface between these two points. The photo below shows a canoe like this, which might be described as having an almost straight keel, and certainly one that manufacturers and canoeists would say has little rocker. If you were to grab hold of one end and try to lift it, there would be literally no longitudinal rocking motion at all.

A brand new 15 foot Mad River Reflection (outside the AS Watersports store in Exeter), which has almost no rocker.

At the other extreme, some canoes have very little of the hull touching the ground, and all of this at the middle. From this mid-point the bottom of the hull rises, before reaching the angle at the bow and stern quite some way off the ground. Given a shove, this canoe (see the photo opposite) would actually rock and, not surprisingly, is described conveniently as having lots of rocker. Canoe makers have mysterious ways of measuring the extent of this rocker with, I imagine, much variation in the methods, but a canoe described as having more than about two inches of rocker has quite a bit. Somewhere between one and two might be average.

So what does this rocker mean in practice?

In simple terms, a canoe with no rocker is easy to paddle in a straight line, while the more rocker you have, the easier the canoe turns. If you imagine a canoe with a pivoting point at the centre, which is convenient because that's where it is, the bow and stern need to shove sideways through a lot of water if the canoe is to be pushed off its straight course. Where there is little or no rocker, there is a lot of hull submerged at these two ends, and a lot of resistance. On the other hand, a canoe with a generous amount of rocker has little if any hull in the water at the ends (just look at the photo of our canoe in the 'Materials' section on page 77), and in turning the resistance is low. In some canoe designs with generous amounts of rocker, particularly when unladen, a 16ft (4.9m) canoe might have only 10 or 12ft (3 to 3.7m) of hull that is actually submerged, and much of that not very deeply. Easy to turn? Yes. Easy to keep in a straight line? No, at least not without a fair bit of practice.

And the best of these two options for canoe camping? Well, as with so many things, I suspect the answer lies somewhere between the two extremes. It is no accident that the majority of canoe models have rocker measurements of 1 to 2ins (2.5 to 5cm).

You can see the rocker quite clearly on this view of our Prospector.

Above waterline profile

In use, this is the bit of the canoe we see. For those susceptible to aesthetic leanings the old adage, 'a line for duty, a curve for beauty', might spring to mind. For me, a good upward sweep of the gunwales to stem and stern lifts the heart as it rises to the sky. Unfortunately, this doesn't necessarily improve the practical characteristics of the canoe. While high ends help keep the water out in choppy conditions, they will also catch the wind. Particularly when unladen, what is a very light vessel sat high out of the water, can certainly be blown about.

The upswept ends and depth of our canoe are obvious here, and probably busy catching any breeze.

This is the same disadvantage of a deep canoe, or put another way, one that has high sides at the mid-point. Anything over around 13ins (33cm) between the base of the hull and the gunwale is a fair bit, and a canoe with centre depth of 15ins (38cm) is naturally more susceptible to 'windage' (the detrimental impact of the wind on a vessel) than one with 13ins, though it will also carry a bigger load. The key to safe canoe camping loading is to see at least 6ins (15cm) of 'freeboard' (the distance between the waterline and top of the gunwales) when the canoe is full. It is easy to see why a Prospector style canoe with 14½ or 15ins (37 to 38cm) of freeboard scores well as a load carrier, until it's empty again of course.

Conclusions

At which point we seem to be back again to considering which canoe is best for the job in hand.

After all this, I'm still tempted to say the one you own. As I mentioned at the start of this section, almost all canoes will do a fairly decent job. It is pretty much what they were developed to do after all. Assuming your canoe isn't particularly long, short or narrow, or put bluntly, extreme in any aspect, it will probably do. In some ways, it is living with some of the failings of a craft in use that will best show you what you don't want.

Perhaps one consideration that has been overlooked is where you intend to paddle, and when. Paddling preferences also need to be considered.

Should your dream be to drift down one of the broad slower-flowing rivers, rarely dealing with anything more serious than the occasional and not very demanding whitewater section, or perhaps to paddle along the edge of a protected lake (but only after checking to see that the weather will be fine for days), then a broad and deep canoe may not be for you. For ease, let average be your benchmark.

To this end, the solo traveller might be looking for a canoe of 15 or 16ft in length (4.8 to 4.9m), two paddlers a craft of 16 or 17ft (4.9 to 5.2m). It will have a beam of about 35ins (89cm) and something close to 1½ins (4cm) of rocker. The centreline depth will measure in at around, or just over, 13ins (33cm). Overall weight might be between 60 and 70lb (27 to 32kg). Hull profiles will be neither particularly rounded or flat-bottomed, with shallow arched being the description to look out for. As conditions are likely to be fairly calm, aesthetics might be indulged, with a satisfying sweep of the gunwales up to the two ends.

This canoe will be big enough and deep enough to carry the kit needed for a reasonable foray in most conditions. It will be easy and enjoyable to paddle, with the gunwale close to the surface and enough hull in the water to ensure that it will track well without deviating from the chosen course, unless you wish it to. It will also be light enough to manhandle from one wet spot to another.

For some campers, and I have to admit it's not for me, the distance covered each day will be what matters. In this case, reducing the rocker will help keep everything in line, and speed will also be improved by choosing a longer vessel.

As with all canoes, the larger the expected load, or the bigger the anticipated waves, the more you'll appreciate a generous centre depth. This will help keep the gunwales away from searching waves. For cargo hauling, particularly over larger bodies of water or wilder rivers, a centre depth of 14 or even 15ins (36 to38cm) might be a good idea. Bow/stern height is a tricky balance though, and remember splash protection comes at the price of windage.

And so to my regular choice of canoe – the Prospector style – considered specifically here, not due to ego, but because it's so popular. In some ways I wish that it

Even when loaded a Prospector has plenty of freeboard (the gap between gunwale and water level) – a very useful quality when the going gets a little rough .

didn't suit me so well. So closely associated is the Prospector with that superstar of canoeing, Bill Mason, that I sometimes almost feel as if I am trespassing. Using a Prospector style canoe certainly does nothing for anyone with individualist tendencies, with almost every other canoe camper out there seeming to be paddling one. Yet there is one very good reason for their popularity, they do the job well – in many circumstances.

But not all, and I make this little point if only in an attempt to stress the benefits of other canoe forms to the camper. My description of the 'average' canoe is not just an idle presentation, but intended as a very definite recommendation, where the expected conditions allow. It is no accident that while singing the praises of his Chestnut Prospector, Bill Mason often chose to use a Pal, from the same manufacturers, when travelling in less demanding situations. Compare the statistics of this fine vessel with my 'average' canoe. The results are intriguing.

Of course once the intended load grew, and most importantly once the chosen river was expected to be wild, then out came Mason's Prospector, at least I suspect that's what happened. Yet even here, we are discussing rivers, where a deep canoe with plenty of rocker allowed the manoeuvrability to cope with more extreme whitewater conditions, while keeping the boat dry. Many will find the enjoyment of lake travel in a Prospector marred severely by its tendency to wander, a result of its generous rocker and high, wind-catching ends.

I choose a canoe with a generous rocker allowance because I like to explore the coastal edge, the more protected coastal edge at least. I've found that in the same way that the Prospector can be manoeuvred easily around swirling and more energetic river settings, it can also be persuaded just as effectively to almost shimmy over confused water and tides, often when they are working in opposition to each other. Great at sea, perhaps not so applicable on a lake, even a big one, with equally big water, where wave trends tend to be less confused. Here a deep canoe with less rocker, that can maintain a straight course with less effort might be more useful.

That's just my choice though, one that suits the loads, usual number of paddlers, and locations most often paddled.

In brief, there is no perfect canoe camping canoe, but knowing when, where and for how long you wish to head off and camp, you can probably track something down that is pretty close.

My last piece of advice, and I suggest an important one – try to paddle in as many canoes as you can before parting with your money. They may all look the same to you (for the moment at least), but they'll almost certainly feel different. And the more you paddle, the greater those differences will seem.

Easy if you have plenty of canoe-owning friends of course. Lots of experimentation (and probably lots of advice too – some even useful). Swamped by paddling pals or not, make sure you also head for a decent canoe shop. You'll soon be able to tell if it is any good, because they'll let you try anything that has caught your eye on the water. Advice is always welcome, but climbing straight from one canoe to another, will often tell you so much more.

Our Prospector – a fine coastal craft, in suitable conditions.

A hole drilled in a plastic boat to take a painter.

Fettling your canoe

Fettling – a lovely term, despite its archaic feel. Instead, I could have used the rather bland 'outfitting' or slightly sensational 'customising'. In short, this is the process of transforming your new canoe from bare vessel to a usable craft. The first step will be to decide how much you want, or importantly need, to add or alter.

At the very least your canoe will need painters, and a length of line (rope) needs to be attached to each end. Suitable painters ensure that you have something to hold onto when not in the canoe, something to assist in manoeuvring it about when not aboard, and, importantly, a means of tying it up securely when it's left on its own. The sight of your vessel bobbing off towards the far horizon on an unaccompanied expedition is not a good one.

This painter job is best served by floating lines, ones that stay on the surface when they fall in (they will fall in). Line of 8 to 10mm diameter is probably best, with a length of anything between 2m and as much as 5m, depending who you talk to. I think something around 3m is plenty, being useful, but not long enough to pose a danger. Anything longer carries the risk of coiling accidentally around something you don't want it to hold onto, such as your leg. Not an obvious danger perhaps, until you imagine it wrapping itself about your ankle during an upset in troubled water.

Using a bowline knot, I tie my painters around the little bow and stern carrying thwarts. A more usual practice, on all canoes constructed from modern synthetic materials at least, is to drill a hole through each end around 8cm in from the stem (and stern) and 6 to 8cm down from the gunwale. The painter can either be threaded through and tied, or a separate line can be looped through, tied on the inside of the canoe, and the painter attached on the outside to that.

In addition to your painter, your canoe fettling minimum requires a bailer. Although specialist items can be bought, this vital safety article need be no more than a bowl or bucket, attached to your canoe either by some line, or my preference, a climber's 'quickdraw' – a short length of strong tape with a karabiner at each end. These quickdraws make secure and easy to release ties for much of the kit that ends up in my canoe.

For me, that's it. If a seat is in the wrong place I'll move it backwards, forwards or up and down a little, but I otherwise manage quite happily with the canoe as it is. The absence of additional tie-in points, often now added to canoes, particularly for camping expeditions, is not something I miss.

A decent bailer.

Part of this relaxed attitude is because for camping trips I don't tend to use additional floatation devices. As will be explained later (page 105) I'm happy to let the load I'm carrying provide this useful buoyancy. This means that extra tie-down points at the bow and stern aren't really needed. I have also developed my own way of tying in our canoe camping gear (page 107), and for this I only need the thwarts provided, with a little help from the bow seat struts. The final reason that some canoeists add attachment points is to assist in the use of splash covers. For a number of reasons, which include a love of simplicity and a slight distrust of things that might get in the way, or even impede an escape in the unpleasant event of a capsized canoe, these don't tend to form part of my rather basic canoe embellishment process either.

All this is personal preference though, and for those that would like to secure extra buoyancy (admittedly useful in an empty boat in rough water), use additional tie-down points, or add splash cover attachments (also helpful when the conditions deteriorate), there are two main options.

Buoyancy bags secured in place.

The first is to attach metal loops or D-rings directly to the canoe's gunwales. These can be either screwed into wooden or deep plastic sections, or, where the plastic is thinner or the gunwales are metal, by drilling holes and using pop-rivets. Positioning for these should soon be obvious, and you can always add a couple more following sea-trials. To keep things tidy, and to avoid rubbing, it might be a good idea, if possible, to place these attachments under the gunwales and out of harm's way. For buoyancy attachment, the aim is to provide lashing points for a latticework of restricting criss-crossed line or tape to hold everything in place.

'Drill and lace' is a term that's often used to describe the second method, and this is best applied to Royalex, plastic and composite vessels. It is quite an invasive process though, and won't suit all for that reason, but it will provide an unbeatable versatility and range of attachment points. For those that might worry about drilling holes all over a boat, in all but the worst conditions they should remain above the waterline (at least most of the time). Besides, if done properly, the lacing process pretty much seals them up anyway.

A canoe fitted with lacing.

The process goes something like this. Purchase the right length of appropriate line – which for a 16ft (4.9m) canoe will be two approximately 5.5m lengths of at least 5mm climber's cord. Using a 5mm drill (or 6mm if using 6mm cord etc.), make holes down the side of the canoe, about 2cm below the gunwale, and 8 to 10cm apart. When deciding on the number of holes, bear in mind that you will want the ends of the cord to finish up inside the canoe. The whole rather unnerving process is made easier by measuring out from a starting point at the centre of the canoe. I suggest beginning with a hole to either side of the centre thwart, using masking tape with ink-drawn points to mark each hole – and don't start drilling until each position is identified and marked. Masking tape has a dual advantage, in that not only can it be moved easily if you think you have it wrong, but it will help stop the drill bit shifting at the start of each cut. Last but not least, take heed of the old carpenters' maxim – "measure twice, cut once". In fact, I'd suggest you mark all the holes with ink-crossed strips of masking tape, check it all, then go off for a cup of tea and then check it all again on your return.

With holes drilled, simply thread the cord through the holes, in and out, and finish with a knot (as I said, on the inside) at each end. At this point you could call it a day, but you can also add lengths of plastic pipe, cut slightly longer than the gap between the holes, and threaded on to chosen points on the inside. The resultant tube-protected cord will not only last longer, but stands proud to facilitate tying. You now have a whole myriad of tying-in positions, both inside and outside the canoe.

Other additions to your canoe can include kneeling thwarts, glued in D-rings and mast mounts and feet, all of which I have absolutely nothing against, but manage without. For example, if I do want to rig a sail, I like to produce everything from scratch, and remove it all again afterwards – and yes, the result probably isn't quite as solid or reliable, but it is just as fun.

Transporting your canoe

I'm not thinking here of the physical bit where you will be required to pick up your trusty vessel and lug it to the water. This is covered under 'The portage' (on page 111). This section considers the longer journey from home to lake, river or sea.

Of course the assumption is that you own a suitable vehicle, and while I'm going to leave it to you to decide whether the city runabout parked cheekily over the double-yellow lines at your door fits the bill, I'm thinking more along the lines of a large saloon, estate car, or better still, a van. All we have to do now is consider the matter of applying you canoe to your wheeled transport, and keeping it there.

A cam strap holding our canoe in place on the van roof.

So happy am I with the system that I use, that this will be the only one I mention.

Following the manufacturer's instructions (of course) add two roof bars to your wheeled steed. It is also best if these bars are designed for the particular steed in question. Within reason, and functionality, try to place these bars as far apart as possible, particularly on a car roof. Extra distance means reduced strain on your canoe, and more stability.

Then you need to add something to those bars to help protect your canoe. This can be either a set of purpose-built foam tubes, with choices available from a number of canoe and kayak accessory manufacturers, or something more homemade, and possibly cheaper. Tubes designed primarily to protect kayaks can sometimes be a little on the short side, particularly if your roof bars are forced close to the wider centre of your canoe, and you may need two at each end. Alternatively buy lengths of foam pipe insulation from a DIY store and tape this in place. Cheap and fairly cheerful it's true, but unless a lot of tape is used, more to protect the foam than to hold it in place, this method is not nearly as long lasting as a dedicated product, and not necessarily so cost-effective in the long run.

Once your vessel is in place, the painters should be tied on at either end. This is achieved easily where old-fashioned towing loops are available, but not nearly so simply on many modern vehicles. All I can suggest here I'm afraid, as vehicles vary so much, is that it is often possible to remove the little plastic covers set into bumpers to allow access to a towing loop, but you will probably need to find something to protect the paintwork from being rubbed by the painter. With all this painter tying, it should be recognised that if the main lashing system is appropriate, tying on the painter should represent no more than a sensible way to get it out of harm's way. It represents only a poor backup should the principal method of securing fail. In summary, I only pull the painter tight enough to stop it flapping. Apart from anything else, I suspect that ratcheting it too tight may well put an unreasonable strain on your canoe.

The main method of security is provided by two purpose-built 5m cam straps. Looped under the roof bar on one side of the canoe, the two ends are passed over the hull, and the non-cam end then threaded under the bar, between the bar end-clamp and the canoe. It can then be threaded through the cam and pulled down tight.

You will be left with a long loose end. This can either be shut into a door, or tied to a bar or the taut(ish) painter.

I promised a comment on lifting your canoe onto the roof, and here it is. For those able to pick up and carry their canoe on their shoulders unassisted (help with this on page 115), it can be propped, bow end up, on the back of the vehicle, and then pushed on fully by lifting and shoving at the stern.

For others with assistance to hand, tip the canoe over, and with a person on either side at the middle (amidships) lift it, upside down, and carry it to the vehicle's stern. The bow can then be tipped up and propped on the rear, possibly even on the rear bar, in the same way, before the stern is lifted and shoved in identical fashion to push the canoe into place. Et voila – off to find some water.

Two people can make light work of lifting a canoe onto a vehicle.

A Grey Owl Scout (and footprints).

A short mention of paddles

This might seem a fairly simple section, and it is, up to point.

Three aspects of paddle choice deserve consideration – material, style and size.

Crudely speaking, paddles come in two main material types – wood, and everything else. It isn't quite as simple as that of course, even when thinking about wood. Which wood? If combining woods, then in what mix?

After all the prevarication about canoes, I'm now going to come straight out with a paddle recommendation, and then try to justify it.

For canoe camping, if you don't already have one, I'd suggest the purchase of a workmanlike wooden paddle, with a fairly spade-like end, made of laminated lime, or what Americans call basswood, the end reinforced with a resin tip. A number of manufacturers make very good examples, and I like the Scout made by Grey Owl. These basic paddles are light, relatively strong, bendy enough in the shaft, and with a modest enough head size to ensure efficiency and comfort over long distances. The resin tip offers welcome protection where it's needed from stone hits and other unintended abuses. They are also not too expensive, warm in the hand and while not nearly as pretty as say a cherrywood ottertail (which make great canoe camping paddles in the hands of the careful and competent user), look suitably traditional (to my mind an important consideration).

Plastic and metal paddles have their place (I'd argue in canoe hire companies or for those intent on hard whitewater use), but lack the feel or look required to satisfy the soul of a canoe camper. As if this isn't enough, I'd also suggest that bent-shaft paddles are best left in the shop, or the hands of the canoe racer.

Fit

Anyone who has spent any time around canoes or canoeists will have come across dozens of slightly different 'sure fire' ways of working out how long a paddle should be for any particular user. These methods involve sitting on chairs, or kneeling, or standing, while lining up particular paddle parts with particular body parts. Some systems work quite well, up to a point, and with the same sort of paddle, but most methods seem to miss the important consideration that it is the length of the shaft that is more important than the length of the paddle as a whole. A 57 inch Ottertail with its long, thin blade is not going to feel like a 57 inch Wenonah Cormorant for example.

I can suggest two ways to find the right length paddle. By far the most effective is to try everyone else's, until you find the one you prefer. This can take rather a long time of course, and does require lots of paddling friends and acquaintances. Next, and assuming you are taking my Grey Owl Scout advice (or similar paddle), I'm going to be particularly hypocritical, and suggest a 'sure fire' method of finding the right size paddle – or at least cutting down the test paddling options considerably.

The 'paddle over the head' sizing method. This one fits me.

In the shop, pick up a Scout (or something like it), curl the fingers of one hand around the top grip as if about to paddle, and the fingers of other around the resin blade end. Then lifting the paddle, and with straight arms out to either side, hold it over your head. If the shaft just touches your head, it's about (note the about) the right size. If the shaft ends up way above your scalp, it's probably (note probably) too short, and if it hits your head, it's probably too long. Once you have your possible size, then take that and try it – properly, adding or taking away an inch or so until you have the paddle for you.

Also bear in mind that a stern paddler often finds a slightly longer paddle suits better than the likely choice of a bow paddler. Anyone paddling solo, and kneeling in the middle, may well want to shorten it a touch too, but then this is not the usual place to paddle a canoe loaded for camping anyway.

Foolproof? Definitely not, but it often works, and certainly cuts down the options.

Scottish spring – often a wonderful time to set out in a canoe with a tent.

How To Take Everything

Water may be wonderful stuff to drink and paddle across, but it can have an irritating habit of creeping in where you don't want it. When it comes to protecting everything you intend to load into your waiting canoe, concerns may focus on a chance immersion in river, lake or sea, but problems are far more likely to come from the stuff falling from the sky.

And the solution in both cases, or at least our solution, dry bags, lots of them.

Storage

With a slight involuntary shudder I well remember those PDB days – Pre Dry Bag that is. Like the Dark Ages, these were times of hardship and stoicism. The wonders of the modern age may have brought us digital photography and touchscreen tablets, but more importantly we can now keep all our camping gear free from damp – and worse.

Quality in dry bags is important, but then there's no need to worry – most of the well-known makers produce perfectly decent offerings, and at the risk of leaving somebody worthy from the list, these include Exped, Sea to Summit, Overboard and good old Ortlieb.

Left: it might be possible to have too many dry bags – but I doubt it.

Right: various dry bags at the centre of a collection of camping gear, including our yellow Ortlieb holdall, and a large, black Ortlieb dry bag filled with our sleeping kit. Here, the Overboard rucksack holds a selection of photographic gear.

Dry bag colour is important though – if only because it makes it so much easier to find things when you need them. As a result of a form of camping natural selection, technology (spare torch batteries, camera leads, a solar charger and the like) tend to end up in a small lime green thing – that I believe may at some point have been purloined from my elder daughter. A pale blue Exped bag usually holds a loo roll (oh so much better when dry). First aid stuff goes in – you've guessed it – a red bag. At least it did until I lost it recently. Just think of all the fun to be had developing your own colour-coded system.

Most of these dry bags are lightweight types. They aren't designed to take much abuse, and are best packed away safely in something else once filled. Although much bulkier, we also have a few big black heavy-duty Ortlieb versions. These are tough enough to take care of themselves.

Sleeping kit

Into one of the larger of these sturdy Ortlieb bags, about 60 litres in capacity, we stuff all our sleeping kit. This includes sleeping bags and pillows, which, all being down filled, really do benefit from being kept dry. Our Thermarest mattresses usually go in here too.

Considering the bulky nature of the contents, it's amazing how tight you can still compress this bag, another benefit of down fillings. Just make one fold of the bag lid, kneel on it all to expel the air, wind in a few more turns, and clip shut.

Clothes

All our clothes end up in either another big, black Ortlieb bag, or a rather nifty holdall version. This holdall benefits from having handles, which help when lugging it about, and compression straps, to reduce its size. Being bright yellow in colour, ours is also easy to spot amongst the predominantly black dry bags and mountain holdalls.

Excellent as these waterproof bags usually are, the material being almost totally trustworthy, the lid closure isn't quite as reliable. This is another reason to aim for the national dry bag collection, and the simple benefits and added security of double-bagging really can't be overstated. Following a good dunking, water may well squeeze its way in between the tightly-rolled lid of one bag, but is unlikely to make it past the second before everything is pulled from the unwanted fluid embrace of river, lake or sea. Before particularly dodgy-looking outings I've been known to triple-bag some dry-loving items, especially cameras.

Cameras

I've only dropped one camera into the drink before now, but one is enough. It's a depressing experience. I'd put the little metal-bodied Fuji compact into a PFD chest pocket, but without employing the sensible addition of closing it properly. It was

I've been known to triple-bag some dry-loving items, especially cameras. Look closely, and you can see a small heavy-duty Ortlieb bag in my hands, and a larger one poking its head out of the Overboard rucksack.

Our red-lidded Curtec pot, doing its protective job.

only as I leant forward to untie the painter from a fence post that it managed to break free, dropping in under my nose, before wobbling down to sit about three foot under, glinting amongst the shingle at the edge of Buttermere.

This might not have been so bad if I'd taken a spare. I hadn't. Amazingly, after sitting it over the hot air outlet on the van's dashboard for a day or two I managed to coax it back into life again. Mind you, I had to experiment for some time before discovering a strange combination of button pressings in order to achieve this. And it never did work again unless you kept a thumb clamped continuously on the picture preview button. Strange I know, but it worked. Some images taken like this were even published.

Of course much the better course of action is to keep your camera above the surface. And while I can't help much with ensuring this in use, other than by suggesting you hold on tight and put a cord or strap around your neck, I might be able to offer some useful hints surrounding transport.

Ideally, some form of purpose-built waterproof case will be used. Pelican boxes spring to mind, and I've used these occasionally, when someone else has paid that is. They come in a range of sizes and shapes, with either slotted foam divides or purpose-built foam cut-outs to suit every delicate mix of cameras, lenses and supporting electronics. Unfortunately, while extremely effective and truly watertight they're also very expensive. Over the years I've met this problem in a few ways.

One of my continuing canoeing rituals is to start almost every trip by dropping my mobile phone and compact camera into a little, white plastic pot made by the Dutch company Curtec. These small watertight containers offer a useful compromise, protecting the smaller stuff at least. Beloved of dinghy sailors, and available, as the advertisement might put it – at all reputable chandleries – it's surprising what will fit in. Even quite a large camera outfit can be shoehorned into one of the six litre ones like ours (a touch fiddly, but far cheaper than a purpose built waterproof case, and so much better than a dripping SLR camera). You will have to devise your own shock-absorption system, but I find a simple liner of high-density foam works well, with individual items often wrapped in their own protective bags. Tried and tested, this small pot remains in use almost every time I push off from the shore.

Where the outfit is too large I have for some time used a roll-top waterproof rucksack made by Overboard, a British company. Good as this is, easy to carry and simple to pack into the canoe, I never fully trust it, and wouldn't expect the manufacturers to either. It's designed to resist water for only shortish periods during shallow dunkings after all. Not quite good enough when high quality photographic kit costs what it does. While I admit to being a little lazy about packing many things away properly on short journeys, I do try hard to stick to something more effective when it comes to my cameras.

So, after being shut away in some suitable form of impact-resistant padded bag, each component – camera, spare lenses, etc. – is then wrapped tightly into an individual dry bag. I also add a large packet of silica gel to each bag, and try to remember to dry them out regularly in the oven. The SLR goes into a robust heavy-duty six litre Ortlieb. It might even go into yet another slightly larger one, the rolltop wound as many times as possible, before finally being deposited in the waterproof rucksack. The opening for this is then also wound tightly and strapped down. I think (hope) this will do the trick, but when I use this system I still have doubts should everything end up submerged for too long.

If, like me, you find concerns remain, either shell out for one of those expensive boxes, make your own, or use a small, plastic olive jar or other form of food barrel. I have to admit that I've never been particularly keen on these food barrels – you know, the big blue plastic ones – for general camping use. I find them a little too bulky and unyielding, but I do acknowledge that they cannot be bettered for protection, both from the damp and knocks. Some of the red-lidded Curtec pots are pretty big, but I was recently given a smallish, blue barrel (see below), which now holds all my kit. Old habits (and fear) still prevail though, and I still put everything in its own dry bag first.

Overboard make a useful dry bag rucksack. Not a bad place for cameras when on the move.

A small, blue-lidded pot is the current home for my camera kit.

Our wannigan (or wineigan), made from two old wine cases.

Food

Given all my water protection concerns so far, Susannah and I are perhaps a little cavalier about our food. I suspect this is because as we carry enough 'emergency' supplies in the form of tins or sealed bags of dried food, all waterproof, that we know that if things did go awry we wouldn't actually starve. There is no denying though that our food boxes, or wannigans as they are often called in the Americas, have never been watertight.

For a long time, our old plastic food box had so many qualities that we felt unable to discard it. Good looks wasn't one of them though. Compared to some of the quite beautiful wooden examples out there, ours was simply utilitarian. In its favour, it slotted, by chance, tight under the central thwart of our Prospector, and it was nearly see-through, so what you needed could be identified without opening the lid. It was also light, fairly robust, and our blue, plastic chopping sheet/board sat neatly within the recessed lid. Last year though, unable to take the plastic any longer, I took a couple of old claret boxes to produce a new wannigan – or is that a wineigan. It seems now to have taken over.

Where foods such as oats or flour really do benefit from dry conditions, these can first go in their own lightweight dry bag or waterproof clip-lidded plastic box.

Despite having mentioned the blue plastic barrel rather dismissively, it has to be acknowledged that, perhaps not surprisingly, they do make good food containers. The 30 litre version would probably be best unless you need to carry a lot of sustenance.

Cooking kit

As cooking kit wouldn't really suffer from a dunking, all our pots, pans, gas-canister stoves and other sundry hardware items, go into a standard Mountain Equipment zipped holdall. The term fits. Candles, oven shelves, axes, saws and the like all end up in here, even our fire irons. Essentially, anything hardy and not afraid of a little damp, much of which finds a use or home around the fire. For those that prefer natural materials, I'm sure a canvas version would be easy to find. For no other reason than habit, our repair kit, secure in yet another dry bag, also goes in here.

One final comment on the cooking kit front concerns tent stoves, the big wood-fired ones that is. Most items you place in a canoe will float, or at least they will once packed properly. This will even work with a stove. For this reason it can be a very good idea to dry bag this piece of kit – not so much to keep it dry (although this precaution can't hurt), but by trapping lots of air in the surrounding bag enough buoyancy should be provided.

This isn't easy, not because it's impossible to find a bag that's big enough, but because it won't last long once in service. These stoves have just too many sharp pointy bits. I have to admit that all this bag-wrecking potential often results in me not bothering, but if you do intend to apply this sensible piece of safety packaging, you can first stash your stove in an old plastic fertilizer bag, or something similar, before slipping it into a good dry bag. Unless your stove is particularly heavy (I'd suggest too heavy), it really will float.

Everything else

Even after dealing with everything mentioned so far, there is still quite a bit to consider.

When planning to travel by canoe, we try to restrict purely personal items to one bag each. Susannah usually uses a small day-bag rucksack and I attempt, and usually fail, to stuff everything I want to carry into an old canvas fishing bag. Much overflow ends up split between various jacket pockets. It still often seems to be tricky to close my bag when it's time to set out, stuffed as it is with binoculars, fire steel, headtorch, spare gloves, hat, Sigg bottle of water, sunglasses, etc. Mind you, it is worth forcing that lid closed. Left unbuckled, I might as well not bother to attach the bag to the canoe at all, leaving it free to float away should it ever end up in the drink.

A rather forlorn picture of a large empty shore-bound blue barrel. As far as my canoe camping goes, the preferred way to see them (but don't let that put you off – really).

As not only cameras need protection, other important items are deposited in our Curtec pot, notably the van key. Up-to-the-minute technology and central-locking may be rather wonderful, but modern wet van keys don't open modern wet van doors. Not a good thing to discover after two or three days spent out somewhere wildish. Joining it in the pot will be our mobile phones. So, in it all goes, before the cheery red lid is screwed down tight and it's clipped to the little stern thwart.

One last idiosyncrasy is our trug. Pulled one summer from the water of Loch Sunnart this wide and flexible plastic bucket, the sort usually used to feed horses, is employed as something of a carry-all. When on the move, it almost always holds our Kelly Kettle. It should also carry matches and some paper or birch bark in, yes you've guessed, another dry bag, and whatever dry fuel we found at the last stop. Even if something useful can nearly always be found to fire up this trusty water heater, it doesn't hurt to have something to fall back on for those rare occasions when nothing comes to hand. Not only does this valuable black plastic addition to our camping kit serve to carry our tea-making kit, but it often helps when gathering firewood, mushrooms and mussels. It even held an injured buzzard once, but that's another story.

Blue barrels

Despite a short mention in the camera section, and an equally brief appearance when discussing food, the blue barrel has so far made little appearance. This might baffle many canoe campers, and probably requires a little explanation – followed by some rectification.

In many ways the qualities of the blue barrel, and my reluctance to use them, are interlinked. All the characteristics that tend to see me shy away – they are hard, unforgiving and rather utilitarian – are exactly the assets that make them so good for carrying anything from pullovers to pasta, and spare maps to spare matches. Available in a range of sizes, the protective qualities are almost unrivalled. Add in the simplicity of the system, and for many campers, two or three blue barrels may well serve to carry everything. In fact, for a large number of canoe campers, they do. And while I don't choose this packing route myself, at least not for all my gear, it should be recalled that I have now selected it for my cameras. These blue tubs work – even if they don't look very pretty while doing it.

A few things to consider though. Blue barrels may well shed rain, but unless you've put it through a good rigorous test don't put too much faith in the lid seal in a full dunking. They're often fine, but not always, especially if used for a long time. I've already mentioned that I still bag each element of my camera kit before it goes in, and you may do well to follow suit, whether storing lenses or leggings. Bagging items also avoids everything being heaped into the barrel in one confusing lump, in which whatever you're after is always the last thing to be revealed.

If you've managed to put your hands on a used barrel, and unless you are absolutely sure what was originally carried in it, err on the safe side, and give it as good a clean as possible. Although often used to carry food, all sorts of other 'interesting' things are also transported in these blue barrels, and not all of them altogether pleasant.

When it comes to carrying your barrel, and depending what's stuffed in there of course, bear in mind that a full 60 litre barrel may well weigh quite a bit. For this reason, two 30 litre versions are often a better bet, and probably much easier to load into your canoe anyway. Also consider employing one of the barrel portage harness systems that allow you to carry the barrel in much the same way as a large, unwieldy rucksack. I admit to no experience here, and I'm sure they help a lot, but I'm still not tempted by what I see. I'll restrict these functional blue barrels to protecting my cameras.

The Isle of Skye.

Canoe packing

Heavy bits in first. Tent, stove, food, and cooking gear (black holdall), all snug and low beneath thwart level, with the weightiest items (in this case the tent and stove) towards the stern.

So, at last, let's imagine ourselves by a west coast Scottish sea loch (always a good place to start). A large pile of assorted dry bags, spare paddles, boxes, and badly folded tarps lie scattered across the shore by your empty canoe. How do we pack it all in?

Low and snug should be the mantra, and key to all good canoe packing is placing the heavy bits at the bottom.

If you have a wood-fired stove, this certainly goes in first. Big tents are usually best off down here too, as are hard-edged things such as food boxes. Those campers using blue barrels need to stow these first too. Thirty litre barrels are easier to slot in than the larger 60 litre versions, for obvious reasons.

Weight should be distributed evenly, both longitudinally and across the canoe. It can be very irritating to push away from the shore, only find a horrendous list (or lean to one side). But then, as your canoe should only be loaded once in the water, as the strain on a boat in being lifted about on land while filled is likely to result in damage, any detrimental results should soon be evident.

I've always found that it helps if I put the tent and any other heavy items behind the centre thwart, or abaft if you prefer the correct nautical terminology. Tucked between this and a stern thwart if you have one, this forms a good basis for weight loading.

A slight bias towards the stern will help steerage. I admit this can sometimes require minor alteration, such as when working into a stiff breeze, when it can help a lot if the balance of weight is just forward of the centre point, but most of the time this loading arrangement is best. Besides, you can usually pull ashore to adjust things easily if the need arises. Practice is the best way to achieve this balance, but you'll soon see if things are wrong when you compare the waterline with the gunwale. Just aim to see the bow a little higher in the water than the stern.

Larger tents usually go in early.

For reasons of stability, try to keep as much as possible below the thwarts. In brief, anything stowed below helps steady your canoe, while anything above will increase any tendency to wobble. The greater the weight of the individual item, the greater the effect. Keeping things low also has the advantage of minimising windage (the detrimental action of wind on your vessel). Unless a helpful breeze lies on your stern, you don't need something acting like a huge sail.

Long skinny things such as spare paddles, fishing rod tubes, and camera tripods can be wedged alongside the lower layers. Light bulky stuff – groundsheets, sleeping bag rolls and the like – can be shipped above the thwarts if need be, tied down tight. If it's likely to rain, the groundsheet can be opened out to offer things below a little extra cover, although as everything should be in dry bags, this is more to help keep water out of the canoe.

Apart from the security of knowing everything will stay dry in rain, all this dry bag usage has another very important benefit that really can't be stressed enough. If

Strapping everything down tight.

water can't get in, air has almost as much trouble sneaking out. Even if packed pretty tight, a lot of this lighter than water stuff will have been trapped amongst clothing, bedding or food. A plastic fishing rod tube offers perhaps six or seven litres of additional buoyancy for example. All very handy if things do ever go awry. It has been claimed before, and I concur – that a canoe packed for camping, using plenty of waterproof containers, and with everything secure, may turn over, but is actually very hard to sink.

As this makes sense to me – and I've tested it – I don't want things to move. I am aware that some people prefer to have everything sat loose in the canoe, tied only to a long line. Set up like this, a capsized canoe can certainly be righted easily. The load can then be pulled to the side and heaved back in – or so the argument goes. This all strikes me as fine – in good conditions, and particularly when the load is small, with not many items. The problem is, the sort of conditions that result in an upset, are just the circumstances in which I don't want a string of bulky items hanging off the canoe. Perhaps it is my liking of coastal travel that leaves me unhappy with is method, but I don't relish finding myself with an upturned canoe, probably in heavy water, a stiff wind or a strong tidal stream, possibly all three – and then having to deal with a giant, lumpy sea anchor. Besides, I will have lost all that natural tied in buoyancy. No, I'll stick to strapping my load in tight until someone can come up with a convincing argument against it.

That being the case, and just to be on the safe side, almost everything I put regularly in a canoe has a climbers' quickdraw clipped to it by one of the two karabiners. This may seem a little extravagant, and these lengths of super-strong tape (sling) with a secure metal attachment at each end aren't cheap, but half a dozen or more make for individual security systems that are oh-so-easy to attach and remove. As I pack everything in, I just clip it into the next item, working the sling under or around a thwart to help. And so to the actual lashing in.

Anyone who enjoys fiddling with ropes and knots needs no encouragement or further explanation from me. If you want to tie in your kit in the traditional manner, please do.

My preference, and one that I find best suits cold and wet fingers, is to employ the 'cam straps' I use to hold the canoe on the roof of the van. Apart from anything else, you will probably already own these useful items, and it saves carrying ever more kit. Threaded though the various box and bag handles and straps, and looped under the odd thwart or around a seat strut, the whole thing can be pulled down tight in an instant, and what's more, stays tight. At the end of the journey it even comes apart again – always a useful characteristic of any tie-down system.

Using cam straps to hold everything in place.

Now just give everything a good check, making sure that no rope or strap ends are loose, posing a potential tangle risk in the case of an upset. Conversely, ensure that your two painters are free. It can be anything between irritating and just plain dangerous to jump for shore, painter in hand, only to find it jamming after no more than a foot or two has pulled loose. In what is almost a final act before setting off, check that your bailer is attached somewhere close to hand, but also in a state in which it can be freed easily if needed.

With everything now tightly in place, final deliberations should focus on freeboard. This is the distance between the water and your gunwales. When loaded, and that includes any paddlers, try to ensure that you still have at least 15cm (6ins) clear. This should guarantee that even if things grow a touch interesting out there, the water you're travelling on should stay largely outside your canoe.

This is the time when a good deep boat such as a Prospector makes so much camping sense.

Plenty of freeboard here (the gap between water and gunwales), and it will still be there even after we've both climbed back in.

On our way.

Making The Most of Your Journey

Planning

Second best to canoe camping is planning to go canoe camping. This is fortunate, as the amount of enjoyment in the field (or on the lake) is often linked directly to the quantity and quality of the preparation, particularly if you are fairly new to the whole wonderful endeavour. Despite the pleasure of all those new experiences, having at least a reasonable idea of what to expect when you arrive can be as important as having everything packed that you might need. The two are also connected of course. I've yet to be disappointed by knowing too much about my intended destination.

By far the best start in gaining this knowledge is …

Well until relatively recently I would, with confidence, have written maps; and while I can't help reaching for my teetering stack of folded and often dog-eared OS and Harvey sheets when considering a new route or destination, I know that things have changed … and keep changing. Which means that almost any specific advice I give here will probably be out of date before this text even reaches the printer.

Our library – guidebooks, and lots of maps. And in case anyone wonders how they're going to fit this into their canoe, don't worry – apart from the correct map for the trip, this lot stays in our van.

What it is safe to say, and may survive at least some passage of time, is that the internet, or whatever it morphs into, is likely to become ever more useful, whether allowing us to view satellite images of the area or route, calculate distances between put-in and camping site, or to read other adventurers' accounts of trips in the same area. We can look up local food stores, fuel stations, flora, fauna, archaeology, weather trends, folk tales and legends ... you get my drift, and if younger than me (reasonably likely) and therefore a digital native rather than a digital convert, you don't need any of this pointing out anyway. Mind you, it's still not that easy to gain access to the web once out there (although this is also likely to change), and when flat batteries and lost signals are also taken into account, you still can't beat taking something wood-pulp based into the wild (in its own little dry bag of course).

After choosing where to go, identifying the best route and all the kit needed to make the most of the experience once there, those new to canoeing often find it hard to decide how far they are likely to travel each day. The put-in point has been determined, but where will you reach by the time light is beginning to fade? This is actually quite hard to answer. So many variables are at play after all. The strength, determination and efficiency of the paddlers, the weight of the load, the natural speed of the boat, and in particular the force and direction of the wind, or on the coast, the tide. The difference in the eventual distance covered between a loaded canoe travelling with or against a stiff breeze will be enormous. Putting 30 kilometres behind you in a day might be quite easy with a following wind. On the next day, if the wind has veered 180 degrees, three kilometres might take almost as long. But then the problem with this question probably shouldn't be how best to answer it, but whether it should be asked at all. Canoe camping isn't a competitive sport after all, or certainly shouldn't be.

If a particular campsite has been identified, then you may need some idea of the likely journey time, but I'm afraid experience is the only real way to achieve a reasonable answer. All I will offer here, is that you aim small to start with, looking for routes of no more than five to ten kilometres. You might even benefit from a first journey or two of less than five to begin with. After all, the distance covered isn't a key factor. And if the voyage is being covered in short order, why not just pull in for a while to take a look at the shoreline along your route. You never know what you might find.

This throws up something to think about when planning route times, which is quite a serious consideration. Imagine that stiff breeze pushing you 30 kilometres to a fine campsite. Then think about the two days, and only two days, you have set aside for your return. Only rarely does the wind also decide to make an about turn to help you on your way. A close look at weather forecasts can help a lot here, but it is always best to anticipate the worst, and not give yourself any sort of paddling marathon when you don't need it. Oh, and make sure to take what you probably feel is too much food on any trip. Far better to have too much, than too little.

As with any journey into the wild, it's a good idea to let someone know where you're going. I'll leave how this is done to you, but a call or text to family or a friend, letting them know where you're heading, and some idea of when you expect to return, is perhaps a minimum.

It probably won't be long before everyone is online, wherever they are.

The portage

Despite the fancy term, no doubt inherited from the French-speaking canoeists of the pioneering Canadian past, this is no more than lugging the canoe, and all your kit, from one place to the other. Regardless of what anyone might say, the portage is rarely a fun part of any canoe camping adventure. Whether just from your van or car to the water (and back), overland between one body of water and another, or, in the classic Canadian scene, along a riverbank to avoid a section of rapids or waterfall, portage distances can vary from short (and sweet) to long (and anything but).

In reality, the epic portages suffered by North Americans on some classic camp trail routes are rarely encountered in Britain. Wild sections of rivers, even in Scotland, are usually fairly short, and you will need to visit the more out of the way parts of Scandinavia to experience (endure) anything similar. In the UK, most of the portages will be from car park to shore – and hopefully not very long. The exceptions will probably be encountered in some of the rugged areas of Scotland, where the canoeist is forced onto dry land to move from river to loch, or from one loch to another. For the record, and only to put things in perspective, the furthest I have portaged a canoe was just over 1.5km, and this with help. On my own I have managed about 1km a couple of times, and would prefer to find ways of avoiding the experience again.

Breaking things down for consideration, we have the canoe, and all that kit. There are also a few irritating practicalities to consider, but we'll come to those later.

The canoe

At least to begin with, if paddling tandem that is, it is probably best to apply teamwork to moving your canoe. Weighing anything between about 25 and 40 kilos, it can be quite a handful on your own – at least at first. It can be done alone though, as discussed soon.

Unless you are expecting flat ground, which I suggest is unlikely, the various forms of clip-, tie- or bolt-on wheeled trolley systems are probably not worth the effort. They will almost certainly be incapable of dealing with the ground in most canoe camping environments, canal routes representing a possible exception – although even here they will be unlikely to help with steps alongside the locks you will be trying to pass. When not in use, which will be the vast bulk of the time, they just get in the way. My suggestion is to carry your canoe.

Before I mention carrying tactics, I feel I should mention 'the slide'. This is not a method I employ very often, and when I do, only over the most appropriate surfaces. On anything but the softest, slipperiest ground, I tend to worry about the potential damage to the hull.

In very basic terms, and it is a very basic system, the slide is just that, pulling, or sliding, your canoe over land. A good cover of damp seaweed allows an almost frictionless (and undamaging) sliding surface, but rarely stretches over a very useful distance. At best it will make a portage from the low tide mark to any beach edge campsite a rare pleasure. I don't slide a canoe over sand.

The slide, on this occasion over wet grass.

Grass, preferably wet grass, is probably OK too, and quite reasonable distances can occasionally be managed. I have also pulled the canoe over that classic mix of heather and low-lying berry bushes, to be found covering vast swathes of the north-western extremities of Europe. Although I have watched canoeists covering quite considerable distances like this in Scotland, and admit to being tempted myself on occasion, I tend to restrict my slides on this surface to no more than a few tens of metres. I feel that even the cheapest plastic canoe deserves some care, and I'm sure this sort of treatment does the boat little good. You will almost inevitably pull it over a hidden stone sooner or later, to say nothing of the gradual impact from (and indeed to) this vegetation, slight as it may seem. Best to pick it up in my book.

Last word on the slide though. If you are going to give it a go, and tempting as it is to use your canoe as a large sled, it can only compound any abrasion damage to the hull if you leave your kit aboard. Again, I see people do this, but I'm far from convinced it's a good idea. There are also the various stresses suffered by the hull itself that worry me too.

When approaching a carry, emptying your canoe properly will also avoid unnecessary and potentially quite damaging tensions on your canoe's structure. One of the easiest ways for two paddlers to carry a canoe, at least to begin with, is simply for each to grab hold of an end, lift, and walk off. In reality the distances that can be covered in this way in comfort are relatively short, but even if it is only a few yards from where the canoe sits on dry land, to where you want it sat in the water, it is best for the structural integrity of your vessel to empty it of all but the lightest items before picking it up.

If I could collect that fabled pound for every time someone has remarked on my strength when they see me pick up our Prospector, I'd … well, I'd buy a new cedar and canvas Prospector. I might make it look easy, but I can assure you I'm not particularly strong. Picking up and carrying a canoe, even quite a heavy one is relatively easy, and it really is all down to technique. Brains (at least a little) not brawn. The problem of course lies in trying to describe and convey such a physical and admittedly odd technique in print, but here goes (helped by the accompanying photos).

Assuming you are right-handed (apologies if not, but this is going to be hard enough to explain as it is – and you only need to reverse everything):

- Stand close alongside the mid-point of your canoe, facing it, with the bow to your left.

- Grab hold of the inner edge of the near gunwale, and lift/pull the canoe to rest at an angle against your legs.

- Take hold of the near end of the centre thwart in your right hand, and now (in one continuous fluid motion), lean back, lift the canoe up onto your thighs, knees bent slightly, reach forward and grab the far side of the thwart with your left hand, pull hard up and towards you, pivoting the canoe against your thighs. As the canoe rises and spins, throw the right arm under the side (this will turn you to face the bow), assisting the canoe as it lifts and rotates, to fall upside down, the thwart across your shoulders.

1. With the bow to the left, lift the canoe to rest against your legs.

2. Grabbing the near end of the centre thwart in your right hand, lift hard, pivoting the canoe against your thighs.

3. As the canoe lifts and spins, reach out and grab the far side of the thwart with your left hand.

4. Still pulling and lifting, throw your right hand under the canoe.

5. Lift and pivot.

6. And there you are.

If this makes sense when first read I'm surprised. The elements are all there of course, but putting them into practice, and making them work, will take repeated reads, and repeated attempts – and many of them will fail I'm sure.

The prop – providing a welcome, sometimes essential, break during a long portage.

All I can say is keep at it. It will work if you persist, and then one day it will all fall into place (or onto your shoulders at least), and you'll be left wondering what all the fuss was about. Now all you need is to work out a way of placing something soft between your neck and that thwart.

On the portage itself, you will be doing extremely well if you can carry even a light canoe for more than a few hundred metres in one go. The trick here, just as you're approaching collapse, is to try to find a suitable tree branch, tree trunk, wall, field gate, narcoleptic deer or even a fence post, in fact anything on which you can prop your canoe to take a breather. Despite my claims that picking a canoe up from the ground is easy, and it is, really, lifting it up from an upside-down propped position is still much better when you're tired.

Alternatives to the basic lift include a variation on the solo theme, and the tandem carry.

If, after repeated attempts, you still find the lift method described above too difficult, one alternative is to stand near the stern or rear thwart, and to lift/spin your vessel over your head in the same way, but while leaving the bow still resting on the ground. This stern lift removes a good third of the weight from the lift, and all that is then needed is a slightly awkward shuffle forward, moving your hands along each gunwale overhead, until you reach the centre thwart – at which point the bow will lift off the ground. Apart from being an easier, if far less elegant, way to end up with a carried canoe, this method is also an excellent way to teach your body the moves needed to accomplish the full lift.

The stern lift.

If you have an assistant, this method can still be adopted, but instead of shuffling forward to the centre thwart, stay where you are to use the rear one instead. Your fellow paddler can then lift the bow and, leaving their head outside the hull, place a gunwale on one shoulder (see the photo below). Quite impressive distances can be covered in this way, and the bow canoe porter can see where they're going, even swapping shoulders easily to reduce the strain. In fact, the stern carrier can also move to the opposing side of the canoe with each swap, also allowing a different part of the neck/shoulders to suffer for a while. As I mentioned, we've covered over 1.5km like this in one go before now.

The shared carry. Much easier than a solo portage.

The kit

Of course all that kit needs to follow the canoe too. This is where shoulder straps on holdalls suddenly look like a very good idea, and anything that resembles a rucksack an even better one. Large dry bags, especially when they are only filled with clothes or sleeping gear, are light enough, and easy enough on the shoulder, to be thrown up and carried there.

This is one of the areas where my slight lack of enthusiasm for large food barrels becomes a little easier to understand. Unless fitted with a good shoulder harness system (note the good) they can be a real trial to carry (although fun to roll if the ground allows).

Left: bags with carrying straps are a very good idea.

Centre: the traditional way to use a tump line – which I don't care much for.

Right: how I prefer to use a tump line to help carry a wannigan – over one shoulder.

Food boxes (wannigans) and stoves also usually prove to be less than entertaining to carry for identical reasons. The 'tump' line system, a long strap (I often use a cam strap) attached securely to allow the weight to be carried on the head (see photo above), may suit. Having once done something unhelpful to my neck while enjoying myself on a motorbike (at least up until that moment anyway), I haven't given this method a go since I was a boy, but I'm sure many will find it works perfectly well.

The last portage issue to mention concerns security, and there is little that can be done about this, particularly when on your own, other than to trust in the goodness of others. It can be hard though to set off over a ridge or through a wood with your canoe while leaving a collection of useful, and often rather expensive, kit lying untended by the shore. Abandoning the canoe to its fate on the return to collect the first bag isn't much fun either. Where there are two in the party, you can either time your trips to cross mid way, reducing the unattended period at either end of the portage, or leave someone permanently with the more inviting looking pile.

Anglers

At this point, chosen I admit because I can't think of a better place for it, I will take the opportunity to mention fishermen (and women).

It is a sad fact that good relations between British anglers and canoeists have not always been guaranteed. Not infrequent scuffles in the past between the two on Loch Maree spring to mind as a sad example. To either a North American canoeist or angler this is extremely baffling, not least because the two are usually found in the same person. Many Canadian or US citizens with a primary interest in fishing will think it second nature to use a canoe to reach any fishy haunt. Likewise, a canoeist over there will as likely take a rod or two with them as a spare hat. A love of nature encompasses both activities with no sense of any artificial division.

As someone whose earliest memories include trying to catch fish, and who has spent many hours by river or sea in the attempt, I also struggle to comprehend the need for animosity – although I do understand many of the reasons.

Along with a myriad of other benefits, the access laws introduced to Scotland in 2005 forced both angler and canoeist to engage in what they should have been doing years ago – talking. Nothing helps any apparent dispute as much as each party finding out what bothers the other. The result – both sides now have a much better idea of what the other hopes to achieve out there, and how, and in almost all cases this simple understanding has resulted in riverside harmony.

Actually, on rounding a headland once on Loch Torridon to see an angler shouting and gesticulating from the bank, I thought I'd come across a rare situation where that harmony had broken down. I paddled over, preparing for what looked to be an inevitable confrontation.

It turned out that, keen to release his favourite lure from the firm embrace of a patch of kelp about 30 metres out, he only wanted to know if I could help. His old Toby returned, I stopped to chat. Not just any old fisherman it turned out. He was a gillie from a famous east coast salmon river. It soon transpired that after significant reservations over the impact that more canoeists would have on his river following the change in law, the actual effect was minimal – possibly beneficial, as once they had been required to sit down and discuss them, both sides had resolved almost all differences. His conclusion – a man who had perhaps 40 years experience on the river – was that he saw no detrimental impact on his beloved fishery at all. Better than that, he was seriously considering buying a canoe himself.

And the conclusion near the end of this rather lengthy detour – if planning a canoe camping tour of a promising river, particularly a favoured salmon river, and the two are very similar, it is worth finding out what any angler you may come across is up to, and how best to limit any disturbance. Of course I see it as the angler's responsibility to do exactly the same with regard to canoeists. We all have an equal right to enjoy these wonderful natural resources after all (or should have), and the last few years seem to prove that it can be done.

On lochs and lakes, common sense suggests that you simply give an angler as much of a wide berth as possible. Not so easy on a river of course. In Scotland, where much of the angling is done from within the river itself, the wading angler will be visible at least. Some bank-side lake fishermen are very hard to spot until you are almost on top of them, or at least their line.

Unfortunately, most anglers fly fishing for salmon or sea trout will be facing down-stream. You might spot them, but they are unlikely to know about your arrival. Most though should be used to canoeists calling out to let them know you're there.

Before long, and it should be no problem to wait for a while (watching a good fly fisherman in action might even impress you), they will let you know on which side you can best pass. Drifting through, using the paddle only to avoid collision is the advised approach. Thankfully these days, a cheery greeting is likely to come first from the rod-wielding wader.

An angler may well not notice you're there.

A very special morning in northern Finland.

Where To Go

Destinations

So where to find your ideal camping location?

Well it has to be acknowledged that in an area as densely populated as England and Wales it's never going to possible to enjoy a true wilderness camping experience. This rather sad recognition is only made worse by a woeful lack of access rights. The simple solution – take my advice and head for Scotland or Scandinavia.

That said, it is possible to have a perfectly good canoe camping experience south of the border, although you will almost invariably have to settle for an official campsite. Waterside offerings can be found for example on the Rivers Wye, Severn and Thames, in amongst the Norfolk Broads, and on the shore of a few of the rather stunning Lakeland meres. Helpful advice regarding routes and formal camping opportunities can be found in Eddie Palmer and Nigel Wilford's *English Canoe Classics* Volumes 1 and 2, by Pesda Press (and a *Welsh Canoe Classics* that I'm told is on its way).

I mentioned Scotland, and since 2005 this stunning and in many parts almost people-free country has boasted access legislation that treats its inhabitants and visitors like adults. It is definitely worth familiarising yourself with the details of the Scottish Access Code before making a visit, but in brief, as long as you don't damage the environment, or impinge either on other people's enjoyment of the land or their ability to work on it, you can do pretty much as you wish on foot and in a canoe. This certainly includes paddling on Scotland's lakes, rivers and coast. Putting up a tent is also allowed just about anywhere you might fancy. As I said, best to check the Code as there are exceptions of course, but these are largely restricted to built up areas (including anyone's garden and school grounds), playing fields or land with crops (and that includes grass for hay or silage). Scots should be very proud.

In discussing Scotland I'm going to avoid being specific about camping locations. In part this is because it would take away from the valid joy of discovery. It is also because Scotland, at least away from the agricultural and busier lowlands, is little short of one huge canoe camping opportunity. Pick almost any inland loch or larger river and, while aware of the limitations just mentioned, you will find somewhere satisfying. In terms of coast, almost anywhere along the western fringe, from the mouth of the Clyde to Cape Wrath, including all those wonderful islands, will offer something special (and besides, hints and clues about specific locations are scattered through

Scotland!

the text and photographs). It really is that good. Combining fair access laws with something very close to real wilderness does nothing less than allow canoe camping in its purest form. Put simply, I couldn't even write this book without Scotland.

And for those wishing to explore beyond our home island?

Canoe camping options in Sweden are just about endless.

Unfortunately, much of Europe is hardly quiet or accessible to wild campers either. Freedom to roam is established in many countries, with boat-able water just as widespread. The ability to put up a tent off the beaten track is less common. With some exceptions, such as the Dordogne in France, where I am told wild camping is tolerated, the farther east or north you travel in Europe the better, on all counts. One area stands out, combining jaw-dropping space with some incredibly mature access arrangements. Scotland provides British canoe campers a chance to exist, Scandinavia offers Europeans genuine wilderness.

Just take Sweden for example. With a long, varied and extremely pretty coast, over 100,000 lakes and scores of beautiful rivers, all set within a country with a vast amount of space, this country is always going to be good.

Not least because of Sweden's Allemansrätten, literally 'all man's right'. This glorious institution, pretty much enshrined within Sweden's very identity, offers some of the most cheery attitudes to access to be found anywhere in the world. In brief, a sensible explorer (and by that I mean one who isn't going to cause damage to wildlife or property) can go almost wherever they want, on land, river or lake, do nearly whatever they want, and at the end of the day, pitch a tent just about anywhere they see fit (well almost). Not surprisingly, there are some limitations. As in Scotland, pitching camp in someone's garden, or the middle of a cultivated field is certainly not acceptable for example. You will also need to purchase a licence to fish or shoot, and while the collection of wild foods and the lighting of fires is allowed, this can only take place if it is done sensibly and without any adverse impact on the land. In the end though, while offering a vital protection to the environment, Allemansrätten aims to allow any responsible traveller a near unfettered right to experience the land.

And then there is Norway.

This approach to access is mirrored in Finland, where it is called Jokamiehenoikeus, and Norway, where Allemannsrett was codified in 1957 with the implementation of the Outdoor Recreation Act. All in all then, the makings of many a perfect canoeing holiday.

Mind you, if you want to use your own vessel, Scandinavia takes some getting to.

Route selection

I am going to assume here that we are talking about wild stuff. If you are heading for a formal campsite the owners should be able to provide assistance in reaching them, from whatever direction you choose.

For those looking for something out of the way, and assuming you are looking at a map of Scotland, somewhere in Scandinavia, or perhaps another gem you've discovered, the key features to identify are put in points and suitable campsites. Unless you have a need to lose weight, the idea of portaging any more than a mile or two, means that most of the many remote lakes, sea lochs and fjords are off limits – certainly the lakes.

Of course one of the advantages of otherwise inaccessible coastal locations is that you can reach them by canoe. Practicalities and safety intervene here though, and I will return to these saltwater journeys just a little later.

Most of the best canoe camping locations are represented by a body of water served by just a single road. This allows the necessary approach with your canoe-crested vehicle, while usually guaranteeing that the lake, loch, river or fjord is not fronted by swathes of houses – or worse.

Rivers need to be big enough to float your canoe at usual water heights.

Rivers need to be big enough to float your canoe at usual water heights, the best being capable of navigation no matter how much water they contain. This usually, but certainly not always, means larger watercourses. For up to the minute information on actual river conditions, the internet or local canoe clubs are often the best source.

Angling websites often have very useful river level information too. Our local river even has a webcam fitted to one of the bridges. Very useful for the keen salmon and sea trout angler, but also for the canoeist wondering whether there is a enough flow to avoid bouncing down the stream from one barely submerged rock to another.

For those not embarking on a river journey, a quick scrutiny of a map will show whether your prospective lake, loch or fjord is free from too much in the way of development. Quite a number of Scottish lochs are still very empty, and numerous Scandinavian examples can usually be found with hardly a house in sight.

Often a stretch of water will have the odd dwelling or settlement along only one side, leaving the opposing bank or shore satisfyingly bare. Of course there may be a good reason for this, and as the morning sun lights up the little white cottages on the distant bank, this may become apparent. Over the long periods involved, experience will have shown which shore benefits from the best weather protection or sun-catching qualities.

Narrow bodies of water are usually safer, and often more interesting.

In fact, when it comes to selecting a specific campsite, especially in Scotland, this wealth of ancient knowledge can often still be put to good use. Along a seemingly desolate and wild shore, it may look as if few have ever set foot on this barren ground, let alone lived there. Look a little closer though, and the stone shell of a small house or two can often be found hidden amongst the bracken. These homes, often abandoned in the face of the cruelty and callousness of late eighteenth and nineteenth century eviction, almost always reveal the prime settlement spots in the area, best sheltered from the wind, and most likely to catch the warmth of the fleeting sun. Find a 'cleared' home and place your tent as near as your sense of trespass will allow. You may thank the skill and judgment of the builder as a storm arrives overnight.

Wiggly, empty shorelines are the preferred option, providing the chance to escape from any weather. The addition of woodland helps on this score, and also in providing firewood of course. Narrow bodies of water are often the most interesting to paddle, with more to see near at hand on either side. Slender lakes or lochs also avoid the need for potentially dangerous crossings of large expanses of open water.

Scotland holds a number of not too broad lochs that offer excellent camping opportunities. In more than a few cases, two or three are connected by canoe-able rivers, or at least watercourses with a bearable number of portage sections. Some lochs are long enough to provide reasonably extended fun on their own, and one rather well-known example, possibly with its own monster, stretches over enough distance to provide a quite decent trip.

For the European canoe camper looking for a genuinely extended trip somewhere at least relatively close to home, Sweden should provide all you could ask for. Often covering considerable distances, a multitude of valleys, particularly those falling south-east from the mountain frontier with Norway offer multi-day camping options. Routes follow watercourses that alternate almost continuously between river and lake, providing almost every (freshwater) water experience imaginable. This is often genuinely wild country though, and even the easier routes are fairly serious propositions. The tougher ones will test the most experienced canoe camper. And then there is Finland. Just look at a map, and the amount of blue ink will tell you all you need to know about the astonishing canoe camping potential of this country.

Islands add interest.

Wherever you travel with your canoe, islands add interest and further opportunities for campsites. Care should be taken though at all wild locations, and particularly islands, not to cause undue disturbance to wildlife, particularly nesting birds or seals with pups. A useful precaution before setting out on your trip might be to contact local wildlife organisations to find out if there are any areas they'd prefer you left unvisited. Loch Maree is an example, where modern access laws have transformed the area, allowing canoeists to venture freely, but where particularly favoured nesting islands are still worth avoiding at certain times of the year.

Care should also be taken to avoid disturbing other people's right to enjoy the land, or importantly, to make a living on it, and it is always best to give any forestry, farming or conservation endeavours as wide a berth as possible. As with fishing, activities such as deer stalking (1st July – 20th October; mostly from August onwards) and grouse shooting (12th August – 10th December) also form an important part of the economy in many rural regions. Between these dates, it would make sense to check where these activities are taking place and to obtain any advice that's on offer. On the edge of a loch or river you're probably never going to get in the way, and besides, nobody should ever shoot where there is any risk of injury beyond the intended target, but you may well wish to venture inland.

Returning to natural phenomena, it is also worth considering prevailing winds. In Britain these come from the south-west. As a rule then, any lake or loch aligned SW to NE is likely to spend much of its time with at least some sort of breeze working its way along its length. It is worth bearing this in mind – although we all know the journey in which we paddle all day into a south-westerly, before returning next day in the face of just as stiff a breeze from completely the opposite direction. High surrounding mountains provide shelter, but can also result in some unexpectedly strong winds being funnelled down intervening valleys. These can occasionally cross the water from some very odd directions.

On sea lochs and fjords there are also tides to consider.

Any approach to your intended sea loch-side campsite will be made much easier if you time the journey to let these ebbs and flows help. Of course this may mean delaying the off, but as long as there will still be plenty of day left on arrival, it is worth it. In fact there are some narrow or shallow spots – and Caolas Mor on Loch Hourn or the Falls of Lora on Loch Etive spring to mind – where it would not only be hard to make progress against an opposing tide, but would be anything between difficult and downright dangerous. Aim either for slack water at these interesting spots, or the point at which the tide is just moving in your favour.

My last word of caution covers open coast journeys. There are some excellent sea lochs that can be reached only by boat, and those in search of true silence and peace will obviously be attracted. The potential dangers of any attempt to round a headland to reach one of these Arcadian offerings should be obvious, and include all the problems of wind, wave, tide and current already mentioned, just multiplied. If you are intent on making one of these fulfilling journeys, set out only in the calmest of conditions, and only when the meteorologists are promising a lengthy continuation. That radio I listed amongst your safety kit is an essential item here. Despite any understandable enthusiasm you may have to be on the way, it is always best to be on the shore, wishing you were on the water, rather than on the water, fervently wishing you were safe ashore.

Canoeing on open sections of sea can be very rewarding, as this view out from Eilean Shona during a circumnavigation shows. You just need to be particularly vigilant.

Heading back to our tent with some firewood. You can burn quite a bit at this time of year.

What To Do When You Get There

"I drifted about from rock to rock, from stream to stream,

from grove to grove. Where night found me, there I camped."

John Muir, 1838–1914.

Already so dark that it was hard to see the other canoe, let alone the not so distant shore, we nosed our way into the bay. As the bow crunched softly over the sandy shingle of the beach the first part of our canoe camping expedition was over. Now we had to create a home, and hardly too soon.

Perhaps the late afternoon rush up Beinn Trilleachan before setting out had been a bit rash. Fun though, with the summit providing spectacular views out over Loch Etive and the surrounding mountains as a prize. Had it been summer, the sun would still have hovered somewhere an inch or two above the peaks to the west. As it was, a now chill October day was well and truly over. My first offering of advice – try to arrive at your chosen campsite in daylight.

Somewhere sheltered.

Turf is best – even if there isn't much of it.

In the event, the four of us knew what we were doing, each had a headtorch to hand (or brow) and the campsite was familiar. In short time we had the tent up and a fire going. Tea had been brewed and a home-dried spicy vegetable meal sat rehydrated and warming in our largest stainless steel pot. All was well with the world, or at least our little bit of it, but there's no denying it would all have been easier in daylight.

Selecting a campsite

If you know where you're heading, and what to expect when you arrive, these late landings are not so bad. Otherwise, it's probably best to allow plenty of time before sundown in order to search out a good spot. Besides, even if you do know the intended site, you can still pull round the headland, expectant cheer in your heart, only to find it already occupied (not a good feeling at the best of times). With a forced smile and less than convincing wave, we've had to move on down a loch in search of another site before now, but fortunately only a couple of times.

So what makes a good spot? For those seasoned campers this will be easy to answer. In fact, if you've camped much before you can pretty well ignore the next bit. The skills are really no different just because you've arrived by canoe.

Even for those unused to camping it's all fairly simple, and essentially down to basic camping common sense. Somewhere flat, sheltered and dry is best, preferably with a springy grass cover. Before finally plumping for a specific location, particularly if there is any wind, wander around a bit. It's amazing how sheltered some unlikely places can be, and wind is worth avoiding, no matter how good your tent. Nothing can keep you awake like flapping – and if there is any breeze, something always flaps.

It is also worth considering the effect of any wind should the direction in which it is blowing change. You might even have an idea where it will move to if you've checked the weather forecast. At the very least, take a look at the direction from which the prevailing wind will arrive (from the south-west in Britain), and imagine it building and blowing hard from over there.

If you're not fortunate enough to find a turf site, shingle is usually fine, and even sand will do. The problem with sand lies in pegging out your tent. Firm damp stuff is not too bad, but managing to find a good secure purchase for a peg in dry sand is really quite tricky. Waking one night to peer up in slight surprise at a starry sky confirmed that. It also proved wrong my assumption that the wind wouldn't get up before dawn. Susannah and I spent the next half an hour running around the beach in the dark searching for stones or large chunks of driftwood to hold our tent down.

Or somewhere mossy.

If you know you are likely to be camping on sandy or soft soils, special long pegs can be purchased. A few of these are always worth storing amongst your collection. A couple of what are called road pins are also very useful. These long steel rods, sharp at one end, with a curly bit at the other, and usually used to support temporary fencing, can be bought at most large tool stores. They make good tent tethers. They also offer a number of other roles, including fire irons and stove guards. Fairly light, a couple are easy to slip in amongst a canoe load.

Bare rock provides the other end of the problem spectrum. Such sites can be fine though, if a large enough space can be identified, but you will need to find suitable boulders or overhanging branches to provide secure guy rope attachments. Deep cracks in the rock will sometimes hold a peg, or even a road pin (if you're a climber you might be able to use the odd cam or nut).

Shingle will do.

Another obvious key to enjoyable camping is choosing a site that's dry – and importantly, stays dry. Watch out for boggy ground. Sometimes it isn't apparent until you sit or lie down on it. Also be a little wary of rivers or streams. As all whitewater kayakers and fly fishermen know, these can rise and spread surprisingly fast when it rains. Sometimes when the downfall is on distant uplands, the deluge only becomes evident as the pretty little stream you're camped alongside decides to move in. I've seen this happen, fortunately for me from slightly higher ground.

For coastal travellers there are tides to consider. That level spot at the back of the bay may look high, but high enough? Obvious maybe, but then we've come quite close to being washed off a seemingly inaccessible spot by a particularly full spring

And even sand is fine, as long as you use some long pegs (with perhaps the help of a few large stones).

A perfect campsite, on this occasion on the shore of Loch Hourn, Scotland.

tide ourselves before now. I knew this tide would be higher than usual (tide tables are very reliable), and had taken this into account (I thought), but eased that little bit further by a stiff up-the-loch breeze, the most elevated point ended up way beyond the dark ribbon of gently rotting seaweed and twigs, and worryingly close to our tent. Look for these obvious high tide marks and then try to find somewhere at least a good foot or two above.

In summary, the ideal campsite will look something like this – and at this point I will need to focus, as the image I'm conjuring up is rather wonderful and not conducive to concentration.

As you pull around a rocky headland, one that plunges into deep clear water while still protecting the small bay from the prevailing wind, you spot the level grass plateau. This is set about three or four feet above the high tide line on the sandy beach, marked by a mix of bleached dry driftwood and dark seaweed. Tight against this flat spot, again on the upwind side, is a modest area of woodland, the odd dead tree hung up spikily amongst the living. You approach slowly, and as you swing the canoe to let it drift in sideways against the sand, a small bright stream can be seen falling over boulders on the other side, eager to return to the sea.

If I add otters frolicking in the shallows you may feel I'm overdoing it, but I'm pleased to report that this has been the case on more than a few occasions along the west coast of Scotland. For some reason otters never seem much bothered by someone in a canoe.

OK, so not every campsite is going to look like this. You may have to do without the convenient wood or stream, but if you are lucky enough to be somewhere reasonably wild, blessed also with sensible access legislation, then something at least vaguely suitable is usually available.

Tent up, you then need to think about cooking arrangements and other campsite comforts.

A campfire is a very special thing.

The campfire

Sigurd Olson, the American environmentalist and wilderness guide, once likened the memory of past campfires to a string of beads. These memories could be blown upon to bring each wilderness night back to life.

This analogy is very apt, and I can't help picturing these rekindled amber, garnets and rubies. Each fire is a jewel, some prettier than others, some due to circumstances more valuable, but each treasured memory is worth salting away for leaner days ahead.

Such attachment to a humble campfire should hardly come as a surprise. It is after all perhaps the oldest thing of beauty controlled by man. It is certainly a prize that must have been of immense practical importance, providing warmth, a deterrent to predators, a means to cook and sterilise water, to say nothing of its ritual potential, or even its simple aesthetic capacity to please and comfort.

Obtaining that fire initially must have been a case of harnessing and conserving the flaming results of a rare wild occurrence – a lightning strike or perhaps a spark thrown by a falling rock. For those early pyrophiles their treasured gem must have comprised a vulnerable open fire, tended constantly and with great care. Later, as experience and knowledge grew, burning embers, perhaps transported within a tightly wrapped fungus, would provide a more sustainable method of securing that priceless source of heat, protection and cooking capabilities for the community.

And then one day the miracle occurred. Just one extremely special individual, applying intelligence and reasoning based on careful experimentation, managed to create fire for themselves. Who was responsible for this simply incredible event, one of the most momentous in our development? How did they manage it? Where and when did it take place? We can forget any thought of an answer, of course … but we still have the results.

Or do we?

Even an open wood fire in the house is a rarity in our ever more sanitised lives. The simple pleasure of sitting on a damp, chilly, winter evening staring into the unfolding story of flame and glowing embers is very hard to find in the modern home. And if that indoor experience is uncommon, when did you last look into a fire under the stars?

Even for those of us with a passion for outdoor living the campfire is becoming an ever more uncommon joy. As night falls during an expedition into the hills, woods, or along our coast, it is far more likely to encounter someone heating their lightweight rehydrated meal over a gas stove.

Now I understand fully the fragility of the ever more pressed remains of our wildish land, and recognise the sense in some of the arguments put forward in favour of avoiding the use of a fire. In certain locations, and at certain times, I wouldn't dream of setting light to anything. Where bare peaty soils are vulnerable to ignition and almost unimaginable damage, or during protracted periods of drought amongst a tangle of tinder-dry vegetation, the lighting of an open fire would be idiotic, but to never camp again without an open fire – it's unthinkable to me. And of course there should be no reason to have to adopt such draconian measures, so long as a measured and appropriate approach to the use of an open fire is allied to some fundamental skills.

Of course that's where so much of the trouble lies. Along with their increasing rarity, we find the simple skills (and they are simple) needed to create and use a safe, open fire in the wild are often worryingly absent. This results in two interconnected problems – those lacking the necessary skills but, having a sense of responsibility, simply avoid lighting a fire at all, so leaving their use only to people who really shouldn't be allowed anywhere near a birthday cake candle, let alone a bundle of burning wood.

A depressing sight in the wild, along with indiscriminate and thoughtless toilet practices, is the abandoned 'pillock' fire. I doubt I need to explain the term. We all

A wood fire really can make a difference to a campsite.

know the ones, even if we have little experience of outdoor living. Pulling ashore, the sounds, sights and smells of the wild alive about us, we find the remains. A wide burnt area, with singed grass and piles of ash and charcoal, ringed with part-burnt logs, none of which should have been anywhere near a functional fire in the first place. What better way to turn people against fire use outdoors?

Well, the 'brainless pillock' fire, encountered with depressing frequency, and raised to this status by an accompanying collection of melted plastic, torn drinks cans, grease encrusted tin foil and broken glass. While the simple pillock fire almost certainly results from no more than an innocent lack of training, this sort of behaviour is unforgivable. I have often stood in profound sadness in some out of the way corner of the world, faced by one of these eyesores and wondering how anyone could make the effort to reach somewhere so beautiful, and then do this to it.

So what to do? You'd like to use a fire, and benefit from all it has to offer, but you know you lack the skills. As a result, you don't have the confidence to put those aspirations into practice. Well, providing yourself with a useful, safe and thoughtful fire really requires only four main considerations:

1. Location
2. Fuel
3. Successful ignition
4. Use

There are numerous other minor aspects that can be refined with practice, but that sums up the important ones. So …

Location

Along with restriction from regulations (check before you set out to make sure you are actually allowed to light a fire where you're going) and/or common courtesy (nobody wants to sit in someone else's smoke), there are a few places, hinted at above, where a fire really cannot be lit. This is largely to do with avoiding setting light to more than you intended. Partly though, it is about ensuring that the collection of fuel will not deplete the environment. Rotting wood can be extremely important to the local ecology, both as a home and larder for insects and fungi, and ultimately as a means of feeding the soil as its nutrients are returned for the next generation of trees.

At any time when drought has turned the area into a large vegetable crisp, use of a fire is best left to the experts – who may well choose not to light one anyway. Peaty soils, such as the ones found on heaths and moors, should also be avoided, although saying that, areas of bare gravel can often be found, particularly along river or steam edges – for obvious reasons, one of the safest places to light a fire after all.

Wherever you do choose to place your fire, just make sure it is as far away from anything flammable as possible. Also take the opportunity to think about wind direction. It may well change of course, and if you've heard a weather forecast you may even be able to predict this, but it is probably best to position your new fire so that the smoke isn't swirling immediately around your tent or any obvious gathering point – or anybody else's for that matter.

If, after careful consideration, you do choose to put match to tinder, it is worth the trouble of a little preparation, both to boost safety and, importantly, to help ensure that you can leave the area as you found it.

Whether on the shingle or sand of a beach, an exposed riverbank, or within woodland, it is sensible to clear an area. This doesn't require major excavation, just the production of a slight depression on sand, gravel or shingle, or the removal of combustible leaves and other vegetable matter to expose the bare soil in a woodland setting. The aim here is to ensure that any fire you light doesn't end up rather bigger than you intended. The area can also be restored more easily when you're finished.

Shingle provides a good safe location for a fire.

A very useful oak branch, found broken away from a fallen tree. All that's needed is a little axe and saw-assisted dismantling.

No shortage of firewood here, on an island in Lake Sädvajaure in northern Sweden.

Fuel

In a search for appropriate fuel for your fire, ask yourself three things – is what you have the right material, in the right condition, and of the right size?

Once the fire is lit (and I will come to that next) you are likely to be burning wood. Over the years, and for various reasons, I have produced fires using peat, considerable amounts of dead flower, reed or shrub stems, straw, dried cow dung and even dried seaweed, but wood is our principal fuel.

Unless you find yourself somewhere completely unwooded, and there aren't many places like this by water, you should be able to gather fuel fairly easily. Even close to popular sites you can usually locate something useful. Besides, if used properly, a campfire really doesn't need that much fuel anyway.

Living wood should always be avoided. Apart from being an unnecessary vandalism, green growth makes very poor firewood. Windfall is the quarry, and pieces that have been caught up and held off the ground are the real prize – likely to be dry while not yet rotten. Where the woods have been thoroughly 'picked', it is always worth searching the high water line along the coast. We have often cooked for a day or three over nothing other than flotsam. We once camped on an island in the middle of a lake in Sweden that had so much dry wood piled on the shore that I didn't even need to stand to gather suitable fuel. Admittedly, I may have had to lean over and stretch a little on the second day.

The only slight disadvantage with driftwood is that it is often quite old, and the older the wood, the less calorific value (heat producing qualities) it possesses. Conversely, as there is often quite a lot of it, this is rarely a problem. You will just end up using a little more. One suggestion – try to avoid painted (easy to spot) or treated wood, both of which can give off some pretty nasty fumes. Sometimes the treated wood is hard to identify, often only revealing itself through a slight green tinge.

Wood should be collected from the ground. Very occasionally, and only when windfalls are lacking, and you're allowed to, should you extend your search to include standing trees.

If you are forced to use standing timber, first ensure that it is dead. In summer, the lack of leaves is usually all you need to tell. In winter, try this little test. Cut off a sliver of wood from beneath the bark and touch it to your tongue. Live wood, or only recently dead wood, will feel cool, damp and slithery. Dead wood will feel warmer, and importantly, because it has dried out itself, will suck the moisture from your tongue, sometimes even leaving the two stuck together. This stuff will burn nicely. And if cutting standing wood, pick only the smaller examples. This has less impact on your environment, and helps to ensure the other important aspect of your fuel-size.

There is simply no need to burn large pieces of wood on a campfire, either to keep warm, or more importantly for cooking. In cooking a much more efficient heat, and far more control, can be had with twigs or small branches. If you are restricted to the use larger pieces, then split them first. Most firewood for cooking should be not much more than three to five centimetres (an inch or two) in diameter, with slightly larger pieces used to build up embers or slow down the need to stoke. Even then, your fuel shouldn't really be more then five to eight centimetres (two to three inches) wide. Only when the fire is being used simply for heat or drying should larger pieces be employed, and lengths of no more than ten centimetres (four inches) in diameter will be fine.

Of course I haven't mentioned how you should split or cut your wood, and the trite response is carefully. For those with little or no experience of cutting wood with an axe or saw, I strongly advise that you find someone who has, and ask them to show you. If this isn't possible, start small, and make sure that your tools are sharp (believe me, you really are less likely to damage yourself with something that you don't need to force). And much as you may relish the idea of striding into the forest in search of fuel, your trusty axe slung over your shoulder, the use of a good bow saw to cut thin branches into usable lengths is probably a much better move from a body-preservation perspective.

A good piece of driftwood.

Firewood, and a useful collection of tools – a good axe, a bow saw and a folding pruning saw. The pile of wood to the left is driftwood – light, easy to cut, but usually fairly fast burning. The other pile is a real prize, dry but solid oak. This will burn slowly and produce lots of heat.

Left: you see – bow saw work really can be fun.

Right: a boot is often better than a hand to hold a piece of wood steady when sawing.

Even bow saws have an irritating and sometimes painful tendency to jump about though, particularly in the early stages of a cut. I once took a team of budding conservationists deep into a remote wood, following a two hour introduction to bow saw use. Despite the course, I decided to warn everyone once again about the skittish nature of the blade before we started work, reminding them all that we were probably an hour from the nearest casualty unit – a good hour as we began to prove only seconds later. For this reason a booted foot is almost always better than a hand to hold a branch in place.

Despite this tendency to skittishness, the bow saw is still a very valuable tool, and when the timber you've found is too thick to use as it is, by far the best way to split it is to saw it into logs first. Try to avoid being too ambitious though, at least to start with. Until you've had plenty of practice, pick branches or tree trunks of no more than about 15cm (6ins) in diameter. A better limit might be 10cm (4ins) at first. These can be cut into logs that vary in length. Thinner pieces can be sawn into rods of up to 30cm (12ins) or so. Broader or knotty timber will sometimes need to be cut quite a bit shorter if the resultant logs are going to split easily.

You will then need to turn to your axe or knife for the splitting itself, with the knife only really an option for quite small pieces. So, to your axe.

First things first – you will need to find a solid splitting platform. This can be either a broad log used on end, or a longer log, with a sizeable flat surface, laid on its side. Just make sure it's good and stable, and placed on the ground at a good distance from other campers. Apart from the obvious dangers from swinging axes, wood has a tendency to spring about a bit during this work. A decent platform reduces the effort needed to split a log by removing that energy-wasting bounce you'll experience if trying to hit a log on bare ground. It also ensures that if you miss your log, or the splitting stroke works, your axe blade hits wood rather than soil, or worse, stones.

Splitting wood with an axe. Note the solid splitting platform, and the fact that the wood is placed on the far side. Any wayward axe then has more platform to hit.

Of course worse still is hitting yourself. Fortunately, there are a few ways that you can reduce that nasty possibility. One of the most effective is to drop down on one knee. This should ensure that when the axe head misses (and it is inevitably when, not if), it has more chance of hitting the ground or splitting platform than you. This is one of the reasons, hinted at in an earlier discussion, why an axe with a longer shaft is often safer in the hands of a novice than a short-handled hatchet.

To further reduce the risk of self-harm, a log placed on the ground in front of your knees (see the photo opposite) also provides an obvious axe head resistant and pain-reducing barrier.

There are of course a number of ways to split wood with an axe, with methods to some extent varying depending on the size of the wood to be split.

Broader, and hopefully shorter, logs can be stood on end and struck cleanly. It makes sense though to place the log at the point farthest from you on your splitting platform. This should ensure that any wayward stroke hits the platform and not the ground, or worse, something with nerve endings. Some wood types, such as ash, will split more easily than others, and with almost all logs, if you can differentiate the thinner end from the broader one, striking this is usually more effective.

Splitting wood with a hatchet. To reduce the chance of hitting myself, I've dropped to one knee, and placed a long log as a barrier.

Left: lifting the log with the axe.

Centre: turning the axe upside down.

Right: horizontal splitting – only really effective with easy to split wood, such as ash.

Rather than simply taking aim and swinging, you can instead choose to use only as much downward force as is needed to 'stick' the blade in the top of the log. This can then be lifted, attached to the axe head and the whole lot brought down again onto your timber-splitting surface (left photo). With perhaps repeated strikes, the head should force its way into the log, causing it to pop apart. This isn't a method I recommend as a primary approach, but may well be inevitable when your axe becomes stuck.

Alternatively, you could adopt a splitting method that takes any power and literally turns it on its head. Once the axe is stuck securely in the top of the log, turn everything upside down, axe and log, and strike the splitting base with the back (poll) of the axe head (centre photo). This will force the log down onto the upturned axe head, again splitting it. A number of strikes may well be needed before it gives in. One drawback to this method is that the log can be quite unwieldy up there above the axe, and for this reason this is a method best applied only to the smaller bits.

A much more controlled, and therefore preferable, way to deal with thinner branches, hopefully cut slightly long, is to hold them out in one hand almost horizontally from the body, laying the far end on the splitting platform (right photo). The blade of our axe can then be held against the wood at the point where it is to be split. Both are lifted together, the stick in one hand, the axe in the other, and then brought down hard against the platform. This method is a little tricky to master, and only really works well with clean-splitting wood, but it is very controlled and probably represents the safest option where the wood allows.

In the absence of an axe, and for smaller diameter pieces of wood, you can use your knife for splitting. Your knife will need to be well made though, with a full tang, and preferably with a fairly thick blade.

With an easy splitting wood such as ash, especially if there are no knots, logs up to 10cm (4ins) in diameter may be attempted. This is ambitious though, and you'd almost certainly be better off, at least at the start, with thinner stuff. Whatever size you consider worth a try, make sure that your knife blade is a good couple of centimetres (or about an inch) longer than the log's diameter. The reason for this should soon become clear. For knife splitting, you will also need a suitable wood baton, approximately 30cm (12ins) long and 4 to 5cm (2ins) wide. For those in the know, hazel is good. If you are planning to try to split any wide logs (over 8cm or 3ins) it is also probably a good idea to cut a triangular wedge from a round piece of hardwood first, using your knife to shape a good, smooth surface on both sides.

Again in a half-kneeling position (it is safer), place your narrow log upright on the timber splitting base. Holding the knife horizontal, use the baton on the back of the blade to tap/knock the section nearest the handle into the upper end, often splitting the log before it is fully embedded.

Should the back of the blade be driven in flush, and the log is still putting up some resistance, knock the blade down further by hitting it with the baton opposite the handle. Hit the blade as close to the log as possible, using pressure from your other hand on the knife handle to counteract the blows. Down goes the blade until the log gives in.

A warning though – it doesn't always work, and the knife may need to be worked/dragged/wriggled free. If this proves impossible, use your wooden wedge, which

Splitting wood with a knife – in this case a fairly short blade means a fairly slender piece of wood.

I carry a fire steel, but light probably 95% of my fires with something from a matchbox. Here are both, with the dry bag I store them in.

Birch bark. My favourite fire lighting (tinder) material.

can be driven into the split with your baton. Alternatively, saw carefully through the log just below where your knife is stuck (but taking care to miss it of course). The log usually splits as you reach the section under the partial crack.

Better still, carry and use an axe.

Successful ignition

Flint and steel, fire-lighting bows and other mysteries of the fire lighting art are all very well, and great fun for the initiated, but I suggest that if you want to feel some warmth and add some colour to your sausages, you use a box of matches or a lighter. I carry a fire steel as a means of insurance, and even use it every now and again, but light probably 95% of my fires with a match.

While you can use old man's beard, carbonised linen, bulrush down, feathers, pine needles and a host of other natural 'tinders' to light a fire, there is really nothing wrong with scrunched up paper – if you have it. If there is one 'traditional' material I would like to draw to the attention of the budding fire lighter, it is birch bark. This quite amazing material, which can also be used to build things as diverse as canoes and teacups, is filled with extraordinarily flammable natural oil made up of a mix of strange things with names such as guaiacol, cresol, creosol, xylenol and phenols. Whatever they're called they burn well. Birch bark is by far my favourite fire lighting medium.

Although I can use a knife to scrap a little nest of birch bark shavings, setting light to this featherlight pile with a lusty spark from my trusty steel, forget all that for the moment. Just collect some silver birch bark (dry bark from dead branches is best, although perfectly good wispy dry bits can be pulled from live wood without causing harm) and hold a lit match near the thinnest papery edge. You will now have fire.

While there are all manner of minor fire-lighting strategies and tactics to discover, and learning them will be fun, start with the basics. Make sure you have a good bundle of very thin completely dry stuff. This can be wood shavings, broken twigs, leaves, dried cow parsley stems or bracken – in fact almost any vegetation that

Left: birch bark on a small mat of dry sticks.

Right: with the very smallest stuff at the bottom, build your pile. This is just the start, and you will need to add two to three times this amount before turning to your matches.

is wispy and dead (and therefore dehydrated). Use these to build something that looks like a messy bird nest, preferably on a flat level mat of dry sticks. This mat will help keep your tinder dry, insulate the baby fire from the cold ground below, and will itself burn to provide a good bed of embers quickly.

With the very smallest stuff at the bottom, build your pile. None of this kindling should be thicker than a pencil, much of it a lot slimmer, with the thinnest stuff low down next to your tinder. While building, try to think like a flame. Make sure there is enough room for this flame to move and search, and for the all-important air to get in. At the same time, ensure that the pile is not so loose that the flame has nothing to bite into. Judging this will take a little practice. Before long you'll be thinking like a flame whenever you see someone start a fire.

Before turning to your matchbox or lighter, make sure you have plenty more thin, dry stuff to add once the flame catches hold. When the time arrives to put match to tinder, you may well have to shield this stage from any wind, which always seems to appear as soon as the matchbox is slid open. This shield can often be provided simply by using your own body, but available bags, boxes, or even the canoe might need to be employed if things are cutting up rough.

Sometimes it may need a little blow.

Use

Once lit, don't be in a rush to lob on any big stuff. Just add slightly larger twigs, chopped small branches or split wood, working gently as the fire starts to take hold. Don't be put off if, after the first burst of flame, things die back a little. Be

For cooking, try to keep firewood small.

Going well, and plenty of flame from an established fire is good for fast frying and boiling.

patient, and should things grow a little too unenthusiastic, a gentle blow, aimed at the brightest glow within the pile, will probably turn things around. Just watch your eyebrows when it works. A useful trick here, to avoid a lungful of smoke, is to turn your head away for each inhalation.

If you plan to cook, wait until you have a good bed of embers (not just flaming wood) before starting. In terms of size, your fire really shouldn't ever be much larger than the base of your cooking vessel.

If you want a pot and pan on the go at the same time, extend the fire in one direction to sit beneath both, without making it any wider. The means by which you prop your cooking vessels over your fire is discussed below.

And when you have finished with your fire? Well make sure all the little stub ends of your fuel, the ones lying around the edge, are pushed up onto the embers to burn through completely. This will ensure that the work needed to clean up your campsite is lessened. Your aim must always be to leave your site as you found it, and advice is given in the section 'Finishing with your campfire' below.

The only time I feel tempted to leave any sign of my presence is at popular campsites with a regularly-used fire pit. At these times it is thoughtful to leave some cut kindling and fuel in a neat pile alongside. It can be very pleasant to arrive tired at your campsite in the evening to discover such a present. Impressively, experience suggests that at least some other campers seem to agree.

So good luck. To master the campfire takes time and practice, but to achieve a working competence shouldn't take long at all, and then you're away. Light, warmth and tasty food that lasts as long as supplies hold out. Or you could add to them so satisfactorily with a little foraging or fishing. The use of a campfire, if practised responsibly, is environmentally friendly and free.

Then there is the simple, yet profoundly satisfying pleasure, of just staring into the results. Go on – find a sensible spot, collect some tinder and kindling, and string your first jewel.

A good cooking fire need only be the size of the pots you want to heat.

Cooking over a campfire

Key to this important skill is fuel control and fire size. I've mentioned size, and the benefits of a small fire can't be over emphasised. A fire that heats your pot, and not everything else within the immediate vicinity is fuel efficient, easy to manage, and much easier to clear up when you strike camp.

Holding your chosen cooking vessel over your fire can be achieved in a number of ways, from the traditional tripod to my favourite fire-irons, perhaps with the addition of an old wire cooker shelf.

The tripod system is fun, and if properly set up allows for easy control of pot position in relation to the heat source. Three suitable poles are often easily found (roughly the same height as you), lashed together at one end, and set out over the fire. You can either use a traditional forked and notched pole to hold the pot, or instead employ a length of flexible wire. Much easier, and this isn't cheating. I think my trick

Left: a tripod in use to boil our small Primus kettle.

Right: a simple wire hook and a length of lightweight chain makes an effective height adjustment system with a tripod.

is even better, using a short length of light chain and two wire hooks (which can be stored in the lidded pot or kettle). One hook holds the pot at the bottom, the other hangs on the string or cord, binding the three poles together. The height of the pot over the fire can be adjusted, depending which chain link is hung over the top hook.

One old and very sensible method was to use two lengths of metal, propped horizontally over the fire on a pair of conveniently placed stones. In short, fire irons. The steel road pins I mentioned will do here, but angle iron is even better, being much more stable (60 to 80cm lengths of 20mm x 20mm x 3mm mild steel work well). In use, pans of different sizes can be accommodated easily by angling the bars to place the ends sat on one stone closer than the other. When finished with, this system also has the advantage of being simple to transport.

A version of this method is to replace the two bars with a large wire shelf, gleaned easily from any abandoned cooker. Ours has a chromed finish, making it easy to

Fire irons in action.

clean. In use, its area defines and restricts the working size of the underlying fire. It is good for cooking food such as fish, meat, or toast straight over the fire.

Better still, you can combine both methods, slipping the shelf over the fire irons when grilling is the aim.

Selecting the right prop stones can take a little time. Occasionally, I've read guides to camping where the use of stones around a fire is frowned upon. Concerns are raised over rocks splitting or being discoloured. I've never experienced the former, but then my fires are small and the stones rarely positioned tight in amongst the action anyway. As for discolouration, I'm not sure. Again, I've not noticed a problem, with any dark colour seemingly caused only by sooting, and soon washed off. I may be wrong here of course, and suspect that prolonged high heats may result in both problems. Best that you keep an eye on this, and adjust your methods accordingly. Where no suitable stones are available, I have used log sections, pushing them into the fire and replacing them as they burn through. Unless you also want

Using an old wire oven shelf to help cook mackerel.

Combining fire irons and an old wire cooker shelf to cook cod and chips in Norway.

any open fire for heat, the blaze is usually short-lived. Where you do want a fire to burn longer, for heat, insect repellence, or just because it looks pretty, the stones can be pulled out of harms way.

Not only should a fire be small, fed with modest fuel as described above, but the best cooking conditions, at least where temperature control is needed, are definitely provided by glowing embers. Flaming wood is fine for boiling water or fast frying, but all other cooking benefits from a good shimmering bed. This may mean that you have to wait some time, rarely less than quarter of an hour, before you have optimum chef-satisfying conditions. I still underestimate this delay every now and again, usually when I've chosen to cook a good, fresh, fishy lunch on a small beach as the tide is coming in. I haven't lost a meal yet, but it has been close.

Using the canoe as a windbreak while cooking in northern Sweden.

How and what to cook

If determined and resourceful, pretty much anything can be cooked over, in, or alongside a wood-fuelled fire, using just about any method. Our ancestors, for example, built stone or wood and clay-lined pits, filled them with water, added a large hunk of meat, and then kept the water simmering for hours by dropping in stones heated in an adjoining fire. The cool ones were then lifted out, before being heated once more in the fire, over and over again. Where there's a will …

To cover the more usual day-to-day cooking requirements though, a wood fire is probably best suited to boiling, frying and grilling, and a huge range of satisfying meals can be produced with just a frying pan and a saucepan full of water.

Possibly seventy-five percent of our dinners start with a sliced onion added to olive oil in one, with pasta, rice or potatoes bubbling in the other. Most of the remainder will represent some form of one-pot broth, casserole or stew. Where we break from this routine it will be to either grill fish directly over the embers, or to bake them in foil – often with lemon or wild fennel.

Something sweet to end the meal is often provided by simmering fruit with a little water and sugar in one pan, while warming custard in another. It is very rare that we travel far into the wild without a few tins of Devon custard. For a bit of variety, we may make up a sweet bannock mix, often with sliced apple, cooking this in an open frying pan.

Whenever anyone writes about canoe camp cooking for more than a few paragraphs, it seems almost inevitable that the subject of bannock will soon turn up. In Canada, where most canoe camping must take place every year, bannock is something of a convention, and passions can sometimes run strong when discussing key ingredients and cooking methods. In fact, even though the indigenous American tribes almost certainly made flat, unleavened bread long before being joined by all us Europeans, bannock is a Scots word, so British canoe campers should feel completely confident in applying their cooking skills to its production without a sense that they've pinched something from overseas.

Camp meals don't need to be dull. Leek and chorizo risotto, produced in Arctic Sweden, using only a frying pan and this MSR saucepan.

Most of our meals probably start with a fried onion, or three.

Simmering fruit in a little water and sugar can produce something sweet.

One of our apple bannocks (and chocolate custard).

Pancakes, with blueberries from the nearby wood.

These round flat pan-cooked breads are almost a canoe camping cliché then, but like the Tilley Hat, only because they suit the activity so well. Either sweet, as mentioned, or savoury, they are simple to cook from only a few easy to carry ingredients, and the results are tasty and filling.

In order to dodge brickbats I was tempted to avoid offering any guidance on bannock constituent parts or cooking methods. I suspect that almost anything I write will render me a marked man. The other reason, and perhaps not very convincing, is that we don't really stick to any one recipe anyway, often experimenting or just working with what we have. That said, you won't go far wrong if you start with:

- 2 mugs of plain flour (we tend to stick to white, but you don't have to)

- 2 teaspoons or so of baking powder (you can leave this out if using self-raising flour)

- ½ teaspoon of salt

- About a mug of milky liquid (roughly half and half milk and water, or milk powder mixed in water)

If you use milk powder, perhaps a mug full, you can mix the dry ingredients before setting out, storing them in an airtight container and simply adding water at the campsite.

Either way, you could also add an egg if you like (reducing the liquid volume a little), but the basic version will do. This can be cooked as it is, and eaten on its own or with your main meal, or you could add fruit and/or honey or sugar if you feel the need for something sweet. Sometimes we add a little cinnamon to the apple version.

Mix everything you've chosen together to form a soft dough, adding a little more liquid if it feels a touch firm. If in doubt, err on the slightly gooey side. This can then be shaped into a slightly smaller than frying pan sized disc.

To cook, pour a generous dollop of vegetable oil into your frying pan, heat it a little and slide in your bannock. Keeping everything away from a high heat (best over embers and avoiding flames) let it sizzle gently for a while. It should rise a touch, and you can turn it after a while (you'll have to guess, or peek under the edge) to let the other side brown too. To be sure that it's cooked through, a knife shoved into the centre, should come out clean, or at least only oily. Then enjoy, while I await the emails, letters and phone calls telling me where I've gone wrong.

Of course, while frying, boiling and grilling probably best suit a wood fire, other key methods can often be applied equally effectively, if involving a little more effort. While you may not wish to simmer a haunch of venison in a pit, the appeal of baking proper bread or cakes in a Dutch or reflector oven may be strong. Sometimes some of the most enjoyable elements of canoe camping can be found in spending enough time in one spot to engage in some dedicated cookery experimentation. Food preparation skills can be pushed, and resourcefulness applied, in devising or attempting new techniques.

At the end of the meal, if washing up liquid is in short supply, fatty pans can be cleaned using a little wood ash. This produces a natural and very effective instant soap. Just be careful though, the resultant ash/water mix removes fat so well because it's surprisingly caustic.

Finishing with your campfire

One final word, or words, relating to your fire – and this concerns finishing with it.

Whether using an established site, or one that leaves you feeling as if you've been the first to ever use it, the ideal with all wood fires is to leave your campsite without it being obvious you've had one there at all. To this end, it does help if all the wood you've used is burnt through. Not only is it a good idea then to sit around your fire once you've finished cooking, gently pushing any twiggy escapees back into the embers, but it can provide a pleasant contemplative way to end the day, meal or visit.

Keeping up with the demand for fuel.

If you are in a bit of a hurry, any hanging about and poking sticks in amongst the glowing stuff will be kept much shorter if you took my advice and kept your fuel small. Used properly, all that will remain will be a surprisingly small pile of grey ash.

Now at an established and regularly visited site this will do. You will almost certainly have used a pit that has been employed many times over, and this small pile of ash will have no detrimental effect on it being used many times over again. Remember, you are leaving the pit as found. Before leaving though, poke about in these ashes, pouring a little water on anything that still glows or smokes. Then check it again. Only when you are completely sure that it is stone cold (use your hand to check for warmth – well you are sure it's out after all) should it be left.

At that wild spot you've found, things are slightly different. In some cases I still think that it's fine to leave things as they are. This includes lunchtime fires on the beach where the next tide is going to remove any remains. As I rarely light a fire anywhere other than on sand or shingle, the first decent rain (in the UK about half an hour later) should wash pretty much all of this away anyway. If I'm expecting an imminent deluge I may leave things. Otherwise, if in doubt, I will dig a slight hollow alongside, shove it in and cover it over.

In the very rare cases where I light a fire on bare ground, and only once I am sure the fire is well and truly out, I take the ash and scatter it about as thinly as needed to make it almost impossible to see. This small amount of ash and charcoal shouldn't be disruptive to most woodland ecosystems, and of course if your fire was a sensible size, there should be very little left anyway. Finally, replace any loose topsoil, and vegetation you may have removed before starting.

Once completed, step back and feel smug in the knowledge that even you can hardly see where you've been.

Stove cooking

Much as I love wood fires, I would be most unhappy if I thought anyone choosing to use a modern stove ended up feeling that they were in any way failing as a canoe camper.

Given everything I've said, it would be silly to suggest that I wouldn't be delighted to see everyone experience what an open fire has to offer, but I'd far prefer they went camping with a canoe and used gas or liquid fuelled stove to cook, than to not set out with a tent in their boat at all. For various reasons you might never use an open fire. So be it. Much as I've argued their merits, stove use is quicker, easier, far less smoky and often the only sensible cooking choice anyway.

Where we do use a gas stove, we often ship a double-ring camping model with quite a large bottle of gas. Heavy it's true, but it won't run dry.

It is also very useful to have those two rings. I've emphasised the fact a canoe camper doesn't need to be restricted to using a small backpackers' stove, and if you are going to choose a larger 'family' version, you may as well have one that allows you to cook in two pans at the same time. As mentioned, most of our meals, some of them quite involved, are produced with just a frying pan and accompanying saucepan.

Try to select a stove that comes with decent-sized burners. A good level of flame adjustment is also important. In reality, it might be quite difficult to keep the flame alight at low settings out there, but with a little shelter for the stove, the ability to turn the heat right down makes many forms of cooking much easier. Small backpackers' stoves are not often very good at this, and, with the small area of flame, burnt food is often the result. A good stove with plenty of control and generous heat producing areas will help considerably in avoiding this.

When cooking on turf, and if your stove doesn't come with legs to keep it off the ground, it might be a good idea to prop it up on some good stable stones (you can see these in the photo above). Perhaps I'm being oversensitive, but it can be

Cooking on a double-ring gas stove.

Wood-fired stove cooking.

a touch depressing to find an out of the way yet still popular campsite, where the position of each recently used stove is marked by a circular area of scorched grass.

And when you've finished cooking on your bottled fuel stove, that's it – no concerns over clearing up.

Wood-fired stove cooking

There's really not that much that needs to be said about cooking on a wood-fired stove that's any different from preparing food on anything else. As with all wood-fuelled cooking, the drier the wood the better, and if you need a quick burst of heat, stoke with small pieces.

Almost all wood stove hotplates will have one end or area that is routinely hotter than the other. This is usually individual to each stove or stove type, and will require some experimentation.

When you have finished with your stove, and if you're using a popular site, the cold ash contents can be tipped into a nearby fire pit. Where an existing pit is absent, but you are by the sea, either scatter the ashes below the high tide line on the beach, or bury them in a pit dug in the sand or shingle. The same burial method can be employed inland, but it may be best just to scatter the ash widely, but only after making sure it is not still hot or containing any embers of course. This may seem cavalier, but if spread widely, the impact on any spot is minimal.

Stove guards

Fire irons being used as stove guards.

In cold and/or wet weather, wood-burning stoves are great in an appropriate tent. One potential risk however, is rolling onto them while asleep. The implications of an inhabited sleeping bag meeting hot steel don't bear thinking about. Lengths of wood, stuck like cricket wickets between slumberers and stove, are a good idea, but even then I worry about these flammable guards being pressed close. This is where those road pins, or even fire irons, can come in handy again.

Sometimes it just won't stop raining.

General campsite hints

Of course many tricks to deal with wet or cold weather are relevant to any of your time spent outside, but are discussed here as the campsite is where a lot of it is likely to be spent. Some suggestions are very much campsite specific.

Dealing with wet

Sometimes it just won't stop raining. It is on these occasions that the benefits of good wet weather clothing are most obvious and welcome. Even with the wonders of modern wet weather garments, if it just doesn't stop, and especially when you add a constant wind, the damp can still get in. At these trying times, there is not much that can be offered in the way of advice on the clothes front, other than to suggest that you have dry alternatives packed away.

These prolonged periods of precipitation are when a good wood-burning tent stove really comes into its own, being as useful in wet weather as a dryer, as it is in cold weather to keep you warm. Not such a good idea at warmer times of year of course, and of little help to those without a tent that can take one.

At these times however, careful use of a fire, sheltered by a tarp awning or large tent porch can provide many of the same drying benefits. It should almost go without saying that any use of an open fire under canvas, even open-sided canvas, needs to be approached with the greatest care. In brief, keep the fire small, and try not to leave it untended.

In wet weather an awning will not only provide shelter for a clothes-drying fire, but can also offer an extremely welcome refuge for damp campers. An awning can be particularly important if, for whatever reason, you are using a small tent. And for those confined, due to cost, to a tiny primary shelter, the relatively small outlay for a waterproof sheet or tarp of some sort will make a disproportionally big difference to the enjoyment of a campsite in prolonged bad weather.

Tarps

Ideally, if you're carrying one, your tarp will be relatively heavy duty, although if well secured, even a very lightweight fabric awning will do. The trick to all this is in that tethering.

A tarp, set up using whatever was to hand – in this case birch branches from the nearby wood, paddles, cam straps, and throw ropes.

Practice makes perfect when it comes to tarp use, and methods will inevitably need to be adapted depending on local topography and the prevailing weather. A campsite situated near suitable trees is obviously the best bet, allowing plenty of attachment and hanging options. Even a single tree makes a good start though, complemented by the use of a pole or poles. Where nothing upright and stable is to hand, dedicated 'tent' poles will be needed. These can be made on location using available natural materials, or even from paddles or fishing rod tubes. To fashion a stable structure, just make sure you use plenty of guy ropes, with lines set at good wide angles to cover every possible direction of strain. The photo below shows the effective use of guy ropes.

Tarp architecture can be extremely varied, but it is probably fairly safe to suggest that you focus on providing enough height for ease of use and comfort, while still providing reasonable weather protection. One edge pegged to, or near, the ground on the side of the prevailing wind, with the other sides open, may well be ideal. It is also important to rig the centre so that it is held a little higher than the rest of the 'roof'. This arrangement will shed rain and allow some headroom. Keep experimenting though.

A climber's quickdraw, pressed into service as a short guy rope.

The addition of a mosquito net is a must in order to turn a tarp into a usable sleeping shelter in northern Sweden.

Some campers find that a good tarp is pretty much all they need in terms of a shelter. Teamed with a decent groundsheet, this form of primary shelter can be great fun, and certainly puts you in touch with your immediate environment.

Mind you, this might not be the ideal solution in areas subject to clouds of particularly hungry flying insects, although the prudent addition of a good mosquito net may solve the problem.

A tarp also makes a good groundsheet for a tent that doesn't have one built in.

Dealing with cold

For many, restricting their canoe camping exploits to the summer months will do, and I have no complaints. I'm just very pleased you're getting out there at all.

Others may feel tempted to extend their camping season into autumn, or to start in spring, taking the chance that amongst the cooler wetter bits, some very fine weather can often be found. Some will also set out in winter, and if cold weather isn't experienced in early spring or late autumn, it certainly will be between November and March. Things obviously become more serious the farther north you travel, and Scotland can produce some exceptionally chilly weather at times in winter.

Saying this, winter canoe camping is actually not only possible, but even enjoyable, if suitably prepared.

Much of the potential discomfort from cold weather can be removed with warm clothing and a good meal, but the devil is in the detail.

Clothes

As long as you're eating something pretty hearty at regular intervals throughout the day, ensuring all that heat-producing internal chemical reaction is well fuelled, all you need then consider is ways to keep that warmth in. I certainly feel a lot warmer with something on my head. A hat can make a big difference, and one that I can pull down over my ears is always welcome.

When it's cold, and this is Scotland in January, a good hat can make quite a difference, especially if it covers your ears and neck.

A Polar Buff, doing its bit.

Something insulating around the neck can also make a big difference. Traditional scarves are all very well, but always seem to come undone at just the wrong moment. During the colder months my almost omnipresent Buff will be supplemented by one of their 'Polar' versions – the name speaking for itself.

I'm lucky. As long as I keep the middle bit of me warm, the extremities, hands and feet, seem to stay that way too. I rarely wear gloves, but when conditions dictate, they can be very welcome. And when I do pull on a pair, it is good if they can stay dry. Mountaineering gloves with waterproof liners are perhaps best, and I recommend finding a pair that allows a thin, inner set to be worn as well. Being able to take the outer pair off to work on something fiddly, while still having some protection for the hands is good. In particularly cold weather, I have a preference for waterproof mittens. Not great for dexterity, but if you wear thin inner gloves, preferably windproof ones, you have the best of both worlds.

At the other end of the body, good socks are an obvious boon. Nice thick pairs made from an expensive mix of wool and something elastic are my favourite. In really cold weather I start with a thin wool pair, then pull something chunkier over the top. The main trick is to ensure that they stay dry.

If you have a tent stove, one of the key benefits is the ability to dry socks when necessary, or any other garment for that matter. Even if your footwear is fully waterproof, and the temperatures are low, feet can still be very sweaty. The benefits from removing this moisture before pulling socks back on in the morning can't be overstated. The immediate sensation is improved, and importantly, these dry socks will be much more effective.

For the body, layering is the trick, or put simply using a number of thin items of clothing rather than one or two thick ones. You probably know all this already, but so effective is layering in keeping in body heat that it merits repetition. The other key element to all this is clothing that breathes and which moves (or wicks) any moisture (rain or perspiration) away from your body. Ideally, in cold conditions, you should avoid exerting yourself to the point where you perspire. Perspiration is no more than dampness after all, and damp means cooling. Easier said than done of course. The perfect balance is clothing that traps warmth without holding that chill-inducing perspiration. Whether you choose natural fibres such as wool, or synthetic versions is up to you, just avoid cotton, which has no place in any cold weather clothing collection.

For what it's worth, I always wear a merino T-shirt. I turn to a long-sleeved version if the temperatures drop still further, and pull both on if it grows very cold, adding a thin wool jumper as a top cover (cashmere is best, being surprisingly tough, although also horribly expensive). If still chilly, on goes a thick woolly jumper (usually made in Norway by such companies as Dale – Susannah's sweater maker of preference, Devold or Norwool). When windy I add a cotton smock to keep all the warmth in place, only turning to a modern coat with a waterproof and breathable membrane such as Gore-Tex if it looks likely to throw it down. Legs tend to see just a pair of modern quick-drying outdoor trousers, with a waterproof layer pulled on top if I grow chilly. Again, I'm fortunate in having legs that seem to have been grown for a kilt, and they rarely seem to feel the cold – if my torso, or body core, is warm that is. For those without Scottish lower limbs, some form of leggings (again best in my opinion when made from merino) under your trousers will help a lot.

A good woolly jumper, keeping me warm as I collect seaweed.

The last mention of clothes in cold weather is to say that I don't take them off when I go to bed, at least not all of them. When temperatures are on the low side, in fact even when they are not that bad, I keep trousers and at least the merino and thinner wool layer on. For some reason I hate sleeping in socks, but if you feel the cold, keeping these on is probably a good idea too.

At night

One thing about official sleeping bag classifications, not always made apparent, is that the various comfort temperatures indicated on the label are based on laboratory tests undertaken with clothed sleepers. Go to bed naked in a temperature of -2°C, in a bag that is rated to be comfortable at -2°C, and you won't be... comfortable that is. You will need at least some level of additional insulation in the form of clothing. In colder weather I also keep my hat on. This is possibly one of the best ways to achieve a decent night's sleep while winter camping. Because it is both very light and very warm, I also replace my heavy jumper with a modern Primaloft-filled smock when the mercury really plummets. I have an old Rab Generator that I almost think of as cold camping nightwear.

These days, I also never contemplate sleeping without a good mat, preferably a Thermarest or similar. Anything that separates you from the ground when sleeping is vital in cold conditions. If, for whatever reason, you find yourself without a mat, spread out anything that provides even a thin intervening layer – clothes, empty bags, spare groundsheets, even empty cardboard food boxes. No matter how small, they will help. If pushed, bracken, dried grass, even twigs or thin branches (preferably with some form of protective layer such as a tarp pulled over the top) will do a surprising amount of good, although watch out for ticks in some areas.

Modern sleeping bags can be very good, but like any piece of high-tech kit (and they are), you'll extract the best performance if they are tuned and used properly. The difference in warmth retention that can be obtained by shaking the bag out

Keeping hydrated in colder weather.

fully when it comes out of the confines of its dry bag can be marked. Make sure you fluff up the down or synthetic insulation fully, allowing all those filaments, natural or otherwise, to do their job properly. Once inside, to obtain the best results, you won't be surprised to hear that zipping it up completely will help. I mention this only because so many people seem to overlook this vital move. This battening down of the hatches includes ensuring that any internal baffles are also closed up. Many modern bags have an inner pull-tight closure that provides a warmth-retaining seal around the shoulders – in effect providing double the insulation at the opening. Some bags have a baffle along the inside of the main zip, and this is worth checking to see that it's in place. Tightening the hood around your face, leaving just your eyes, nose and mouth free helps enormously too. You shouldn't have to wait long before the temperature rises. All this 'getting in' effectively can take a little practice, made so much easier with someone to help, but it really pays to learn how to get it right. Snug as a bug and all that.

One thing to avoid, and I mention this because it is so easy to do, is breathing into your sleeping bag. Tempting as it is to enjoy the warmth of your breath inside the bag, and it does seem to help for a while, staying like this for any length of time with your mouth inside can produce damp from your breath that will start to work against you. In fact, with down-filled sleeping bags, the damage done to the insulating qualities of the feathers can apparently be quite serious.

If you are camping in any sort of cold weather it also pays dividends to eat something warm before going to bed. Fuel again. The benefits can't be overstated.

Keeping hydrated also helps your body heat itself. Here though, the benefits will need to be balanced against the chance that too much hot chocolate may prompt an unwelcome need to leave your cosy sleeping bag, and tent, at some point during the night.

On the rare occasions during the day when I do feel the cold I have a slightly annoying habit (for others that is) of running around until I feel warm again. This can also be a very good idea immediately before hitting your sleeping bag too. Start the night warm, and you have a much better chance of staying that way.

Dealing with breakages and repairs

Some people are naturals when it comes to mending things in the wild (possibly even looking forward to something useful giving way). Others are not. Even the keenest 'mender' will struggle though without a reasonably full emergency repair kit, so I hope this sometimes vital bag is somewhere to hand amongst the camping kit.

Long, thin things, such as paddles, tent poles and the like, can usually be splinted, using something of a similar shape and size from your kit collection. Alternatively, a branch, or even a piece of driftwood off the beach, will probably do. Duct tape, plastic pull ties, or both, depending on the need for strength, can be used to bind it all in place. One of our modern, flexible tent poles was once repaired very effectively, with the help of a plastic marker pen body, found on the side of a track, and held in place over the break with duct tape. It lasted for the full week of the trip.

Flat things that 'develop' holes or splits – but that don't need to be heated – such as jackets, dry bags or even the sides of canoes, can usually be mended with duct tape alone. Remember that a clean, dry, grease-free surface is essential, and warming the tape will really help. It can often be useful to place a patch on both sides, particularly on fabrics where the hole is large enough to allow the two sticky faces to 'weld' together.

Left: duct tape repairs to a jacket. Good as new.

Right: a repair to our Kelly Kettle base (it had seen a lot of hard use), cut from an abandoned sheet of corrugated iron.

Non-flexible things can often be revitalised with Araldite, using a patch cut from something lying on the shore or beach if needed. One slight word of warning here, if planning to slice up one of the worryingly large number of plastic bottles or containers washed up. Give some thought to what they may once have held. This can range from distilled water or shampoo to bleach, or worse. I have seen someone burnt quite badly just by handling an innocent-looking plastic bottle.

This warning having been made, it has to be stressed that some very useful repair materials can often be found on a beach, lakeshore or even the roadside. In rare and happy cases, substitutes can sometimes be lifted straight from the sand or shingle. Broken guy ropes can be replaced by untangling a lost net, or old fishing line. These have often provided a strong binding for something broken before now. You never know quite what useful thing you might find.

If something that needs to be heated, such as a pan, develops a fault, wire can often save the day. I've mentioned it already, but a small pair of pliers or one of the Leatherman-type multi-tools can make the production of a tight twist in the wire so much easier. The spikey bit on a Swiss Army knife can bore holes in some surprisingly tough materials, even aluminium, allowing wire to be used to stitch things together.

You might even end up with something useful. Note the small folding saw – very useful for initial cutting down.

Other campsite activities

If truthful, I suspect that this short section is only here to allow me to mention whittling. If there is one campsite activity beyond pitching a tent and feeding ourselves that represents a link between us occasional campers and our ancestors who did it as a way of life, it is the working and carving of wood. If you accept my argument, it allows us to forge a yet deeper connection with those early communities and at the same time encourages much more familiarity with the trees in the surrounding environment – each of which produces wood with different qualities. Wood-carving, or whittling, is therapeutic, and a very good way to fill a long winter evening. There is also a reasonable chance that something useful will be produced at the end of the process.

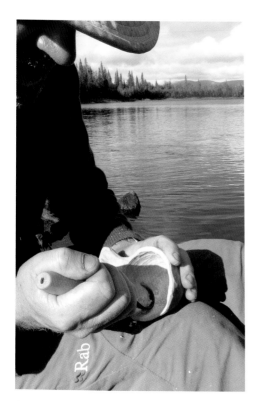

A spoon knife in action.

As a minimum, all that is needed is an axe and a good knife, both of which I'd suggest you should already have. Add a small saw (I prefer the folding type, and you may well already be carrying this in your canoe already) and a specialist spoon knife, and you are ready to make anything from a butter knife to a coffee mug. No matter how suspect the results of first attempt, I'm pretty certain you'll be pleased with it.

I'll leave you to delve further into this woodland art, but to set you on your way, go in search of some silver birch, preferably a length that has just fallen and is therefore still fresh and green. That way you won't have to fell anything either. Cut yourself a section with as few side branches and knots as possible, and start paring. My only other suggestion – keep those tool edges sharp.

What to do when you leave

So you're almost packed and ready to go, either moving on to somewhere new or about to make that sometimes less than cheery return to civilisation. The fire has been dealt with and everything is in bags or boxes awaiting a reunion with your canoe.

Even at little bays or sandy strands accessible only by water, I've sometimes found a surprising amount of junk on some sites. I suspect it arrived by powerboat, or at least that's what I like to tell myself.

Often though it isn't rubbish or an ugly fire pit that I come across at a site, but a tin opener, hat or hairbrush.

It's amazing how easy it is to leave things behind. 'One last look around' has become almost a mantra of our campsite departures … and it's worth it. Our last visit to Loch Etive in Scotland saw us come very close to leaving without my thirty-year-old pair of waxed mittens. Despite both of us having given the whole area some pretty careful scrutiny, I'd still failed to look that little farther out beyond the immediate campsite. I'd only put the mittens on because we wanted to be away soon, and the stove chimney had been still too warm to handle. Once well clear of the tent, hot pipes dropped, I'd deposited my hand protection on a mitten-coloured log. I would have missed them, and a last look around has often turned up a tent peg or hair band.

Susannah once lost a favourite green Buff. We know exactly where, because we spotted it lying on the shingle – in a photograph though, two days later and a day's drive away.

One last look around.

Enjoying a northern Swedish late summer sunset from the best seat available.

Beyond The Campsite

So you've managed to wangle some time away from work, you've packed for the off, then repacked a few times, checking and rechecking that you have everything. You, or at least your car or van, has lugged your canoe along many miles of horrendously busy motorway, your eyes glued to the road. You've found your river, lake or chosen stretch of protected coast. Tired arms attest to the hours of paddling to reach your campsite, and skinned knees, scratched calves and a burnt thumb illustrate the effort put into creating a fine new home. Now what?

Walking and clambering

A pretty obvious suggestion really. You can of course see plenty from the canoe, but having found what may be a rather wild and out of the way place, it makes sense, at least to me, to set out on foot to explore. You can either stick to the shore or head inland. It's probably going to be very beautiful whichever way you choose.

You don't need me to tell you what to look for either. I just like to wander, often uphill, simply enjoying the space, and marvelling at the beauty of the available geology, flora and fauna.

All locked and safe (hopefully). Using a surfboard security cable.

To make this easier, and safer, I like to take along a good pair of walking boots and a rucksack. Both will usually fit easily on board. If my map covering the watery bits falls short, I'll also carry something that takes in the land alongside. To make the most of what's on offer I usually have a lightweight pair of binoculars around my neck.

If you plan to indulge in anything a little more adventurous than light hillwalking, particularly in winter conditions, you'll need quite a bit more kit. Then again, if you are contemplating this sort of activity, the aim itself suggests experience, and you therefore don't need my advice.

One problem with pedestrian exploration is canoe and campsite security. Even in the wildest of spots it can be a little alarming to leave everything untended as you set out for the hills. The ideal solution is to have someone in the party who doesn't see the appeal of setting out on foot. In my experience this is rare though, and for those groups in which each member is susceptible to the allure of high or empty ground, one solution is to take it in turns. This can work particularly well when two couples have travelled in a brace of boats. Even this though can be a little frustrating. It is often much more fun to wander together.

Of course if someone really wants to pinch your stuff, then nothing is going to stop them. I must admit that I rarely leave a campsite untended for long. I have done it in some of the wilder parts of northern Sweden, but out on the tundra, you could see the canoe and tent from miles away.

Where we do want to climb, we usually do this before pitching the tent and setting camp. The best system I've developed for protecting the canoe is to use one of those plastic-covered steel cables, the ones with the plastic ball at one end, used by surfers to protect car-top surfboards (see the photo on the left). Threaded through a thwart or two, thrown around a tree and then secured by a lock through both looped ends, some reasonable security is provided. You can even add a few other things such as pfds to the loop. It is usually possible to find somewhere out of the way to stash other goodies, sometimes covered with stones or dead wood. I haven't forgotten where we put it yet.

Another system for adding security to the more valuable goodies you can't carry with you, is the use of one of the wire-mesh sacks that can be bought at many good outdoor kit shops. Some of these are reasonably big, although also quite expensive. They do offer some form of deterrent. Again not perfect, especially for items that can be wiggled through the gaps, but good for packed tents and holdalls.

Fishing

Looking back I find it hard to picture a time when fishing didn't feature fairly high amongst all the other routine, or not so routine, activities. Each parent and both brothers are keen fly fishers, and my grandfather's family launched themselves onto the North Sea in open boats to make a living catching fish, so this is not perhaps that surprising.

Left: mackerel on a handline off Senja, Norway.

Right: Norwegian cod.

A simple handline setup.

Untangling a handline. My canvas tackle bag is in the canoe.

The result is that very few canoe camping trips, at least at sea, are made without some form of fishing tackle aboard, often including a rod or two. Fortunately these can be shipped fairly easily, and I usually store them in a robust capped plastic tube. All I then take is an old canvas bucket bag, filled with an ever more tangled mess of spare lines, fly boxes, floats and spinners.

Fish can be caught from the shore of course, but in my experience the results are often much better in a canoe, even if only propelled a few yards beyond the usual casting distance. Purpose-built beach casting rods can be abandoned in favour of a shorter lighter version, or even a simple handline. The cost and frustration of tackle lost to weed or rocks can also often be avoided by the simple expedient of paddling just beyond them. A lightweight anchor, especially the easily-stored umbrella type, can be very useful here.

Although I enjoy fly fishing, and spinning, many of the fish I've caught from a canoe have been taken on a handline. Sometimes these are fooled by some choice piece of bait dangled below a float or trundled along the bottom, but perhaps more often by a flashy little spinner trolled behind. It is almost routine for us to offer something gaudy and tempting on the end of a line as we paddle from one beach to another. Left to their own devices these little eye-catching (if you're a fish) contraptions can often improve dinner time. Canoe cruising speeds seem well suited to attract pollock, mackerel and bass. Other canoe catches have included perch and brown trout, and at sea, plaice, sea trout, cod, pouting (and weaver fish!) … and yes, everything you may have read about the pain from a weaver fish sting is true. After my rather too intimate encounter, a small part of my finger eventually went black and fell off.

Sadly, there will never be enough space here to offer anything but the smallest comment on this vast subject, but I think there is room for a brief introduction to handline use.

Take a standard handline (the gaudy combination of orange plastic frame and braided line available at so many seaside shops will do). Tie a brass swivel onto the end of the line, and loop a largish stainless steel clip through the attached eye (see the photo below). This clip, available at most angling stores, can be used to hold a lead weight of suitable size (down to experiment I'm afraid). Attaching the weight here also holds the swivel steady to ensure a twist-free fishing line. Then tie a good long length of stoutish monofilament to the free swivel eye (say 5 to 7kg breaking strain), and then add a spinner to the remaining working end. I suggest trying either silver Mepps or Toby (any decent fishing tackle shop will help with the choice).

Once afloat, and in deep enough weed-free water, chuck it all over the side – or nearly all. Hold on to the frame! Now here are the useful bits. To leave your hands free, after letting out a good length of line (experiment again), put the frame under your foot. And to ensure that the whole lot doesn't go over the side if you should hook something interesting, clip the line above your foot through a large climbing karabiner, itself attached to a thwart. Even if your foot comes off the frame during all the paddling fun, the handline frame can't make it past the karabiner. This saves fish, money and tempers.

Mind you, as mentioned before in the food section, any catch should only ever be seen as an addition to a well stocked camping larder. Try not to rely on angling success to provide a meal. It just doesn't always work out that way.

A last comment about licences and permits. If you wish to fish on a river or lake (which will belong to somebody, or at least the fishing rights will) you will need both a rod licence (available from the Post Office and most fishing tackle shops) and permission from the owner (almost always at a cost).

For the moment there is no need for a rod or fishing license on tidal water – unless fishing for salmon or sea trout. Despite this having been the case throughout history – as far as I know – there are mutterings from those that think they know best (or just want to extract more money from us) that they are considering a change to this relaxed and extremely agreeable situation. For what it's worth, here is my plea that things are left as they are.

Cooking the results.

Foraging

Bearing in the mind the need to consider any nourriture trouvé only as welcome additions to a good store of shipped in food, canoes are ideal vessels to go in search of additional edible goodies. This shouldn't come as a surprise of course, as it is exactly what they were designed to do.

While they also had as many other roles as need and the imagination could conjure up, it was primarily to assist fishing, foraging and hunting that the canoe was developed. Reaching out of the way mussel beds might be just one useful example – as helpful a task off Skye or the Devon coast today as it must have been in what we call Nova Scotia over countless previous centuries.

A canoe could transport you to a remote bank, beach, bay or island that had either escaped the predations of other hungry humans, or just happened to provide the best environment for the healthy growth of plant, fish, fowl or beast. This was vital

A canoe can propel you to places that haven't been picked bare by hungry pedestrians.

to early hunter-gatherer communities, and while few of us campers are likely to starve today if we can't find an untouched bed of mussels or woodland packed with ripe pecan nuts (OK, hazelnuts), we can still benefit from a touch of foraging ourselves. Not only is the chance to rekindle some of these ancient skills enjoyable and valuable in itself, but the results can be pretty pleasant too.

So what's on offer to the peckish canoeist? Well at first glance the inland hunter-gatherer may seem to be at no great advantage from being afloat. With such seemingly unexciting water-edge snacks as bulrushes on the menu, you might feel it worth staying on shore. But then a canoe can also take you to islands dotted with untouched cep, chanterelle, blackberries or wild garlic. It can also propel you to quiet and overgrown sections of lake or river, inaccessible to the land-tied forager or angler. In the same way that the canoe once provided access to areas beyond those picked bare by the hungry pedestrian, today it is possible to reach virtually unvisited sections of shore where elderberries and even rabbits and trout flourish untouched.

Collecting dulse.

Despite all this, it is along and just off the coast that I devote most of my efforts. Once an inbuilt love of the sea is taken into account, there are probably two additional reasons. Firstly, although I enjoy eating trout and even carp, eels and pike, I'd far sooner put something finny on my plate that has spent its days in the salty stuff. And while I prefer the taste of sea fish, I can also go in search of bass, mackerel or plaice without worrying about the rod licences or permits mentioned above. Sea fishing is much more easy-going. All this freedom suits me, and while you can pick and gather all manner of wonders inland, that type of fishing needs paperwork. And then, let's face it, the appallingly limited access to our rivers and lakes in my home country hardly improves the situation. It's not surprising I tend to head for the coast where you have all those maritime delicacies on offer.

Coastal foods can probably be broken down into five basic groups – fish, shellfish, crustaceans, plants and seaweed. A slightly arbitrary list, and open to debate and adjustment no doubt, but isn't that half the fun of lists.

Collecting mussels from north Cornwall.

Fish have been mentioned. For the gathering of all sorts of edible plants, seaweeds and shellfish, the canoe can also take you to the best and hopefully least visited spots, and carry your spoils back to the campsite. I think my favourite meal of this type to date must be bass wrapped in tin foil, their gutty bits replaced with wild fennel from the overhanging cliff top (note – a good knife and a roll of tinfoil already lay amongst my cooking kit. Oh yes, and a lemon).

Mind you there was also a very good brown crab caught close to a low cliff near Torquay. This was memorable perhaps not so much for the resultant meal, which was excellent, as for seeing Susannah race to win her tasty prize. We'd spotted this rather ample crustacean pottering amongst the seaweed across a narrow rock platform about four or five feet down. The problem was that so had a large grey seal swimming through deep water alongside. Susannah took one look at the crab, another at the seal, which made the mistake of hesitating, before she was in and submerged, to resurface moments later with her catch. I'm not sure whether the look on the seal's face showed surprise or admiration.

If bass and brown crab don't do it for you, perhaps the following items on the menu will whet a few appetites – cockles, winkles, shrimps, prawns, the lovely and under-rated razor clam and lobster.

Many edible coastal plants and seaweeds take some cooking, but small amounts of the fresh new growth from sea purslane, sea beet or perennial wall rocket can make a particularly good addition to a salad. Gutweed may not sound very appetising, but is worth the effort (just), and dulse, the easy to identify red seaweed is simple to collect and cook (steam lightly) and really is very enjoyable to eat. Laver, or 'what a paLaver' as it is known in the family, tastes pretty good (although not all agree), but unless you are prepared to hang around a fire or stove for hours until it is properly cooked, using alarming amounts of fuel, it is pretty hard to justify as a campsite meal.

Lovers of a variety of crustaceans will enjoy the ease in which their canoe will put them in touch with remote and rarely foraged shrimp and prawn homes. They are also simple to cook. All that's needed is a suitable net.

A canoe really comes into its own when used to transport a pot or two to a quiet location. Proper crab and lobster pots are fairly big, and it probably won't be possible to take one camping, unless you have an eighteen foot canoe or longer. Best leave these for non-camping trips. Prawn pots are smaller though, especially the canoe-friendly collapsible variety. Not forgetting that prawns won't be found in close to the beach until late spring, and gone again in autumn, a well-placed pot can provide a satisfying meal.

Remember though that there are a shrinking number of hard-hit fishermen trying to make a living from these tasty wee (and not so wee) beasties. Try not to use any spot more than once, at least in any summer. It might be worth attaching a label to your marker buoy or pot explaining this, and the fact that you are only after something for your own table. Sadly, this may still not stop a pot disappearing if you set it out of sight. I suggest laying it within view of your campsite or afternoon picnic spot, with a return within a few hours.

You may think that anything on the shore, or just off it, is fair game, but it's not alas as simple as that, at least in the UK. For a start, all shore or beach is owned by someone

Setting a collapsible prawn pot early in the morning.

Foraging in Scandinavia. Hjortron, or Cloudberries.

– although free access is usually accepted (and this free access is now enshrined in law in Scotland). On the other hand, anyone who tells you that any form of foraging is unlawful, has also got the wrong end of the stick. The truth lies somewhere between the two, wrapped up in all sorts of legal fuss that only British lawyers could sustain, and further complicated by various regional and local rules and byelaws.

What I can say is that collecting plants is fine. Assuming you only cut off a little of each, don't damage them or dig anything up (which rules out sea holly roots for example), and you leave rare things such as wild cabbage alone (well, perhaps the very occasional leaf), plants are on the menu. Seaweed is a grey area (actually, if it is grey don't eat it). While plant collection is fine under common law and statute (fruit, fungi, flowers and foliage are in) seaweed isn't classed as a plant in law, at least in the matter of collection (metaphorical throwing up of hands). Collecting shellfish is classed as fishing, and therefore permissible within tidal waters. Watch out though, bivalves such as oysters and clams, even mussels, are often grown within private fisheries. Best to check. While at it, find out if there are any local byelaws, and check the minimum size limits, closed seasons and even net mesh sizes for shellfish and crustaceans. These too can vary from area to area. Size limits and other restrictions also apply (quite rightly) to many fish, not least the hard hit bass.

On a happier note, foraging in Scandinavia is bound up in far fewer, if any, restrictions – if food is collected for your own use.

While aware that I could put you off trying any of this foraging, and I really don't want to, I must mention the risk of poisoning. Sadly, this is no idle threat, and people really do manage to inflict some nasty mischief on themselves every year, even those who probably should know better. Mistaking hemlock water dropwort for innocent (and I think, overly tasty) alexanders for example is a mistake you'd probably only make once. So the old adage – eat only things that you are absolutely certain about – is one well worth adhering to. The best way to gain this knowledge is to spend a fair bit of time in the wild with someone who knows (really knows) what they are about.

After all this, I must stress that the pleasure to be had from collecting your own food from the wild is well worth it, particularly if you have given your canoe a chance to shine in its true calling. Free camping food can be yours, and extremely good food at that. If you don't have a wild food specialist amongst your friends, the next best approach for increased safety and fun is a collection of good books. If you refer to these constantly, and leave anything you are still even vaguely unsure about, you really should be fine. We bought *Food for Free*, written by Richard Mabey, back so long ago I can't even remember the date. It's a good place to start. Ray Mears (you may have heard of him) can always be relied on. Finally, John Wright's *Edible Seashore*, published in 2009 by Bloomsbury is a star, and I wish I'd had it in a dry bag years ago.

A few additional hints and suggestions:

If you're not sure, don't eat it.

*   Carry lots of bags to avoid everything getting mixed up – plastic keeps everything in the canoe dry and food free, but isn't always the best thing for your catch (fabric bags can breathe).

*   A big plastic bucket is very useful to put your bags in (empty or full) – and also makes a good bailer.

*   A knife or scissors are good for seaweed collection (if you leave the stem, and only take some of the fronds, they can grow you another meal).

*   In the same vein, try to take only a small proportion of any wild food – and find out about size limits and closed seasons (for fish and shellfish).

*   Watch your feet – it is easy to squish things you aren't looking for.

*   With shellfish, stick to the old 'only collect when there's an R in the month' adage (and because canoeing needs you, learn how to clean your shellfish before cooking).

*   At the risk of going on a bit – keep an eye on the tide.

*   And once again for good measure – if you're not sure, don't eat it.

Looking out from the Scottish mainland towards the islands of Eigg and Rum.

How To Stay Safe

Safety on the journey

As a strong believer in people's right to choose for themselves, I have slight reservations about this chapter, but only if anyone reading it assumes I am trying to tell them what to do. Instead, my intention is to put into practice what I believe governments should consider whenever a health or safety matter requires action – to provide as much information as possible, and then leave people to make up their own mind.

Perhaps the best place to start is to look at those risks.

There are risks of course, and other than staying at home, which is the last thing I want to see happen, the best way to meet those hazards is to identify them. Potential risks on the journey can be divided to produce the following two categories:

- Getting lost
- Being injured while afloat

The implications of getting lost are pretty obvious. Put a little bluntly, the main risks afloat can be summarised as follows:

- Hypothermia
- Drowning

A map – and the landscape it shows. Yes, the map is upside down, but I'm looking south.

Always good to have your map easily to hand when on the water …

This all looks a little alarming, and is until you recognise the nature and extent of any problem. Once the risks are understood, by far the most effective response is to try to avoid it happening in the first place (precaution). We can deal with what to do in the unfortunate situation that precaution hasn't worked (response) a little later.

Avoiding getting lost

A rather brilliant lecturer at college enjoyed throwing out unexpected questions. It certainly kept us on our toes. One of his favourite standbys was "What is a map?"

The stock answer, or at least one he'd accept somewhat grudgingly, was "a scaled-down, two-dimensional representation of the earth's surface." A map, however complicated it might look, is no more or less than that. Whatever you stand or paddle on, whether it's a mountain, lake, or riverside, is shown in exactly the same form, on your map, just at a smaller scale. All the main features around you are also shown. You just need to know how to read it.

Your map does need to be well produced of course, and my advice (in the UK) is to stick to those made by either the Ordnance Survey or Harveys. Neither will let you down, and the success and enjoyment of any trip will be enhanced immeasurably by employing one, and better still, by learning how to use it properly.

Basic navigational skills are really quite easy to acquire, particularly if you can count an experienced adventurer amongst your friends. Signing up for a course run by a reputable establishment is an option if you can't. If that's not for you, a thorough introduction to the necessary techniques can be found in a number of books, including Lyle Brotherton's *Ultimate Navigation Manual*.

Not only will these simple skills make your trip much safer, but you can begin to enjoy the journey even before you set off. Anyone familiar with map use has only to look at a decent sheet to see the rise and fall of the fells, to picture the sweep of a loch, almost to feel the salty breeze sweeping up from the sea.

Avoiding injury afloat (precaution)

One of the most effective ways to make travelling in the wild a lot safer is to adopt a certain outdoor outlook or approach. I suppose I should have some impressive name for this adjusted state of mind, but I've never bothered considering one. My concern is also that applying one might run the risk of making a simple mental adjustment sound overly elaborate and unattainable. In reality, all I'm suggesting is a subtle shift in attitude when away from the street and city that raises an awareness of your actions and promotes a little reflection on the potential repercussions.

I admit that, applied over-vigorously, this could be a recipe for ruining your time outside, and I certainly don't want to have anyone fretting over each mundane and everyday move while out and about. What I have in mind is an approach that, before embarking on any new and unfamiliar activity (particularly activities afloat), pro-

Giving the next move a little consideration.

motes just a brief moment to consider the possible outcome. In a way this outlook develops a form of running checklist, in which you ask yourself such questions as:

- Before we set out, is that enough freeboard?

- Have I tidied away any loose ropes or straps on this loaded canoe – but still left the painter accessible?

- Can I reach the bailer from here, and is it secure?

- If we set out across this bay now, can that approaching powerboat see us down here near water level?

- Is this sandbank I'm about to jump onto as firm as it looks?

- Is the wind out here growing too strong?

- Or even – might this be a good moment to pull ashore, and/or turn back?

And most important of all:

- Can I, or my paddling partner, reach shore from here if something should go wrong?

Perhaps as a canoe camping book, this isn't the place to try to cover all potential floating perils. These are best covered fully in a specific canoe handling book, such as *Canoeing* by Ray Goodwin, but for those less experienced canoeists, there are few concerns that I do wish to raise – two relating to all forms of canoe travel, one specific to rivers, and one regarding only those that set out in their canoe along the coast.

The first is connected closely to that question, "Can we reach the shore from here?" Whether on a Lakeland mere, Scottish loch or Norwegian fjord, the danger of misjudging wind and wave size can be equally alarming. Let me set the scene.

You're stood on the shore of a largish expanse of water. Cheer is in your heart because while you need to paddle quite a long way to your intended destination, set way over on the other side; there is a pleasant breeze at your back, one that you feel will inevitably help push you all the way. The sun is out and the water looks perfect, with only the smallest of waves on the surface beyond the canoe's bow. Setting out you hardly need to paddle, that breeze is pushing you along nicely, possibly even building a little as you reach the halfway point.

The problem is, that the waves are starting to build too, helped by the very same breeze – or is it now a light wind? The farther you go the worse it gets. But still, you tell yourself, the far bank is at least approaching, slowly.

Try to avoid a free flight in one of these.

Growing closer, but not that fast, the water below your canoe begins to shallow. Simple physics are now against you. As the depth decreases, the waves grow yet larger. When a particularly strong gust buffets at your back, twisting the canoe a touch, you suddenly realise that the day isn't nearly as pleasant as you thought.

What now? Keep going, the waves lifting and curling white at the crest, or try to turn back? Can you turn back? To turn beam on to these waves is now a very risky business. And those waves are still growing …

In summary, always be very wary of any open water crossing with the wind at your stern. It might seem to be harder work, but setting out into a breeze should ensure that you can see the worst conditions even before setting off. It is also much easier to turn back when you are reasonably confident that you know what lies between you and the shore.

Mention of waves leads on to rivers – and consideration of rapids.

Working your way upstream, you have plenty of time to consider these constricted and often stony sections of river, the water foaming around submerged stones and sudden drops in the riverbed on its journey to the sea. In these situations you can usually pull ashore easily, to peer at the whitewater above and decide whether to

Found at the mouth of a well-known and boisterous river. Something obviousy went horribly wrong here.

portage around, or to pull your vessel along the edge. Travelling downstream is a different matter altogether.

Accidents take place each year at rapids or waterfalls, and they don't necessarily involve those failing in a deliberate attempt to negotiate these exciting stretches of river, as you might expect. Many canoeists who never even intended to run the rapid at all are caught out. While it is usually easy to pull ashore when travelling against the current, it can be much harder when moving with it, especially if the rapid or fall that's just appeared downstream is unexpected.

Prior study of a good map before setting out can often identify some of the larger, rough sections of river, but certainly not all. Depending on your skills in white-water, many disturbed stretches can come as an unpleasant surprise. Learning how to pull ashore on these occasions – and just as important to stay there safely until you've stepped onto dry land – is vital (see *Canoeing* by Ray Goodwin). If you have any doubts about your ability to achieve this, try to find someone to show you.

Just in case you may feel that pulling ashore well upstream of the predicted trouble will do, and while this does make a great deal of sense, it doesn't cover situations where the map fails to indicate the problem. It also doesn't deal with the fact that a map may well also fail to show you that there isn't actually anywhere safe to do this. Be prepared, and know you are capable, when needs be, to turn and paddle back the way you came, sometimes quite a long way.

For those taking their canoe onto the sea, the regular and predictable tidal rises and falls bring more than just a change in water level. As all that wet stuff lifts and drops, it has to push its way over shallow bits or through those narrow sections between one coast and another. As a result, a tide flows, sometimes extremely fast. This can be very helpful if you time your journey and you know how fast it is travelling and in what direction and at what time. Sadly, it can also be quite scary, even dangerous.

In brief, it is probably not a good idea to consider a journey on the salty stuff unless or until all these tides, winds and currents are familiar and understood. I hold the strong conviction that the canoe is a perfectly seaworthy craft – on the right stretches of sea, at the right times, and in the right hands. I suggest though that unless a tick can be placed against all three of these 'rights', it might be best to find somewhere wet to travel inland.

Little doubt about the water temperature here.

My last consideration concerns water temperature. I'm afraid it's a fairly long consideration, but only due to the potential consequences.

You may feel that the dangers of cold water are obvious, but it might be worth taking a closer look at what happens should we be unlucky enough to go over the side – and what can be done to reduce the risks. First though, what do we actually mean by cold water? When is it chilly enough to cause a problem? 10°C perhaps... maybe 5?

In fact, fall into anything below around 25°C when normally clothed, and cooling begins. There's even a risk from hypothermia, although admittedly you'd need to be in there for quite a while for any real threat, and I'm certainly not calling this temperature cold. But the mercury doesn't have to drop much further before hidden dangers can strike – and surprisingly fast.

Submerged, the human body loses heat about 25 times faster than it will in air of the same temperature. Without protective clothing the effects will soon be felt. At around 10°C, even somebody who is reasonably fit could become exhausted, even lose consciousness, in as little as an hour. Despite the warming benefits of the Gulf Stream, Scottish sea loch temperatures often hover around 4 to 7°C in winter. Inland waters may well be quite a few degrees lower still.

At between 5°C and 1°C, or common British winter water temperatures, exhaustion or unconsciousness could strike as quickly as a rather alarming 15 minutes. A lot depends on physical fitness and body makeup, but survival times at these temperatures could be as little as 30 minutes. Not many will last more than an hour and a half.

You may well argue of course that this is still a long time to sort yourself out, to make it ashore or back into your vessel, but these times don't reflect the whole story – far from it.

Immersed at 5 to 10°C, it is estimated that the average canoeist is likely to lose dexterity and most grip strength in less than five minutes. Put a little more bluntly, that's the ability to use your hands. Having an hour or so to affect some sort of self-recovery sounds good, but may not be a great deal of use if you can't hold a rope or grab tight on some convenient bank-side vegetation after a only few minutes. Dressed inadequately and stuck in water below 5°C, fingers can become useless in under three minutes. Closer to freezing and you may well struggle to grasp anything, not least that all-important thrown rope, in less than two.

Worryingly, it doesn't actually have to be that cold for hands to fail. Even in water as warm as 15°C, someone may suffer the same inability to grab that safety line in as many minutes. Southern England sea temperatures rarely rise much above 17 or 18°C, and that's in summer.

If that isn't bad enough, the initial shock from immersion can be anything from disagreeable to deadly, depending on individual vigour, clothing and water temperature. Along with often violent shivering, the instant skin cooling that results from immersion produces an involuntary gasp response (sometimes called the torso reflex) followed by hyperventilation. At best this can be frightening and unpleasant. If you're unlucky enough to have your head held underwater, or waves are breaking across your face, you may not be able to stop yourself breathing in.

Equally nasty, from a whole range of detrimental physical responses, can be the strain on the heart – sometimes a strain the system can't take. Loss of consciousness, obviously not a good thing when swimming, can also occur simply as a result of this sudden and surprise contact with frigid water.

After this initial contact, if you survive it (apologies, but deaths really do occur in these first few minutes), the main danger lies in the loss of mental and physical ability. I've already mentioned what can happen to your hands, but a deterioration in cerebral function can have a serious impact on the way in which vital survival decisions are made – or not made.

Depending on water temperature, a quarter to half an hour or so after going in, it is the cessation of normal bodily functions that poses the real danger. Cold water simply stops you working. The clinical definition of hypothermia is a core temperature below 35°C, but in fact any sustained drop in body temperature can result in this very dangerous condition.

Try not to be fooled by the weather or time of year either. It's all too easy to appreciate the dangers when clouds are dark and low, and the water the colour of old lead, but with the sun beaming down on your Scottish loch from an azure blue, early April sky, it can be very tempting to lose a few layers in the unexpected warmth. Cheery as the whole scene looks, the water is hiding a potentially nasty secret. Fed

The sun might be out, and the air warm, but that water is going to be very cold indeed.

by a few mountains' worth of melting snowfields, it's probably colder in there than at any other time of the year. Put bluntly, a sad number of people who fall into Scottish lochs in spring have a nasty tendency not climb out again. As the old saying goes – *'Dress for the water, not for the air'*.

In short, this means clothing that keeps as much warmth in as possible, and as much water out (or at least restricts its movement). There is something of a pay-off involved here though, with outfits generally becoming gradually less comfortable and versatile as these qualities improve.

I've had my say about the inadequacies of cotton already. It is much better to adopt fabrics that maintain their thermal properties when wet, and this includes modern synthetic textiles, and wool.

Aim for good layering principles. For what it's worth I go for a thin merino base layer (short-sleeved year round, long-sleeved if it's cold, both when really chilly). Over this/these goes a thin cashmere jumper. Yes this is fairly expensive, but also very effective and much more hardwearing than you might think. If I suspect the water temperature is particularly low, then I also pull on a modern insulating smock or good thick jumper (usually Norwegian).

Legs receive a thick pair of winter trousers (usually in some quick-drying, stretchy, synthetic material). On rare occasions a pair of thin thermal leggings go on first.

Over it all, body and legs, goes some sort of waterproof outer shell. This is essential, but less to keep rain out (important as that is) and more to slow the inrush of the cold beastly wet stuff in the case of an upset. Crucially, this impervious layer will also keep that water in place once there, letting it warm up a bit.

A good hill coat or smock and waterproof leggings will do the job pretty well, and also function happily once ashore, but it has to be admitted that something designed specifically for paddlesports will undoubtedly perform better, particularly as these garments usually include a good seal at neck, wrists, waist and ankles.

Unfortunately, they're not so comfy and relaxed around the campfire. Decisions to make, and almost inevitable compromises – or take both.

Don't forget extremities. All pretty obvious perhaps, but a good hat, particularly one that covers the ears and is just tight enough not to fall off easily in an upset is vital. Decent headgear also decreases the impact of that initial thermal shock to the head. Add a Polar Buff to protect the neck, or adopt a Balaclava, and the risk is diminished further, probably significantly. Good gloves, preferably waterproof, will be welcomed (I quite like roomy lightweight gauntlets over a thin windproof pair), and good wool socks will help keep heat escaping from feet. Whether to protect head, neck, hands or feet, various forms of neoprene wetsuit peripherals are worth considering, and I've used gloves and boots in this material.

A day to think particularly carefully about clothing.

The bothy bag. Good and warm in there.

In fact, lightweight modern neoprene is probably worth considering for legs and torso too when conditions are particularly poor. Anything that puts a barrier between your skin and the inrush of cold water must be a good idea. The only problem with this sort of kit is that it is often not very comfortable if worn for the sort of prolonged periods that often go with canoe camping.

Final mention goes to drysuits. In my view not as comfortable as more traditional clothing, but without doubt providing the best form of worn protection. If you're venturing onto really cold water, especially when the air is Arctic too, these admittedly expensive garments will lengthen survival times in the water dramatically. Not only have tests and real-life emergencies consistently shown that those ending up in the water in a drysuit, put bluntly, last very much longer than those dressed even in the next best options, but they help avoid much of the associated pain (and I use that word deliberately). If you are dressed in one of these, the whole overboard experience might not even be that bad. To be fair, they are the preferred winter option for many canoeists.

I mentioned air temperatures, and these do need to be considered carefully. Pull yourself out on a still 5°C day and you'll suffer discomfort. Drag yourself successfully from the same water when the thermometer reads the same 5°C and a strong northerly wind is blowing across the loch, and you may suffer something much worse.

Which is when a dry bag packed with a change of clothing is a vital addition to any canoe load in cold weather. With luck you'll be able to get at it once ashore.

Whether you're still with your upturned/swamped canoe or not, the ability to pull a bothy bag from a coat pocket can provide anything from a little comfort to a longer life. These little wonder-shelters don't weigh much, work just as well when wet, and pack down small. If you have any doubts about their effectiveness, just try eating lunch in one sometime on a cold windy day. The ability to place a chilled or potentially hypothermic colleague, or yourself, somewhere warm is vital. If you have one of these shelters, the job is so much easier. Identification and treatment of hypothermia is dealt with fully in the next chapter, but you won't go wrong if you take anyone who has ended up in cold water and place them somewhere warm as quickly as possible. Bothy bags offer an invaluable assistance in the wild.

If you can get at your canoe, a flask of something hot and a couple of bars of chocolate, packed somewhere for just such an eventuality, won't go amiss either.

Coping when things do go wrong (response)

We've jumped though, somehow reaching the comfort and security of the shore, without considering the nasty, wet, cold and scary bit between going in and this reassuring moment. What about that rather appalling swim?

And the big question – do you stay with your canoe?

Well, Bill Mason once wrote that he'd given the matter a lot of thought, and if clambering back in wasn't possible, he couldn't see the merits unless rescue was close at hand. I'd have to agree – up to a point.

If you have friends afloat nearby, or some other craft is in view, then it's obviously best to stay put. Your canoe will provide something pleasantly buoyant to hang onto, and a visible target for potential rescuers.

If the water is empty though, you can't find a way back into your boat and, crucially, the shore isn't too far away, I'd suggest you consider making for dry land as fast as possible.

But how far is too far?

Well here is something to dwell on. A recent Canadian study by Dr C. Brooks came to the sobering conclusion that even strong swimmers cannot assume that they'll be able to move themselves very far in cold water. In fact, swimming ability in warm water can be seen as no indication of what can be achieved at low temperatures.

When cold, how far is too far? I'd suggest this probably is.

For physically able and fit individuals, even survival is not guaranteed. An example is given of a good swimmer, aged 20, who disappeared while trying to swim only 50 yards from his overturned craft. The water was calm, the temperature around 10°C.

At which unsettling point the most significant cold water canoeing consideration is raised – one that requires contemplation long before ending up in the water – the distance you travel from land. Keep this important question in mind at all times on the water – it's nice and simple – can you swim easily from where you are to somewhere dry? What's more, can you do it when your arms won't work properly, your brain is fast beginning to shut down, and you're struggling even to breathe?

Put another way, how far do you think you'd get. On careful reflection, you may decide it's not very far. That'll probably be about right. This definitely isn't the time of year for crossing open water.

If you do end up overboard try not to panic. Easily said of course, but however difficult to achieve, a clear head could make a big difference when the going suddenly becomes very wet and chilly. Try to evaluate your situation, and any self recovery or swim for shore quickly, but without rushing.

By far the best plan, if you recall how fast the water can suck heat from your body, is to get back into that canoe. If you can pull even only an arm or part of your chest above the surface, the benefit will be marked. Once in, even a swamped canoe is far, far better than no canoe, and can usually be paddled, albeit slowly. Just get out of the water. And if you're at all unsure about self recovery, perhaps you should consider whether you ought to be out there in the first place.

Should you end up in the grim position of having lost contact with your canoe, and making for any shore is unreasonable, it seems most advice is to avoid movement (including swimming), trying to achieve something as close to the foetal position as possible. Well, that's the guidance anyway, although I suspect the urge to try to swim towards anything visible would prevail with me.

All said and done, and despite some fairly alarming content, this section isn't meant to scare you off the water. Far from it, and my only intention is to raise the profile of the potential dangers of travelling in a canoe on cold water so that you can make your own, informed, decisions – the response is up to you.

There really is no reason to avoid canoeing in cold conditions – if properly prepared and within the limits of the weakest member of your party (which might be you, or me). In fact, the chance to explore an otherwise busy expanse of water in the emptiness of winter can be a real privilege. Even in the usually quiet corners, everything is often that bit more special in the stillness of a truly cold, bright winter day.

Perhaps taking the concept to extremes here, but when travelling over cold water it is always best to stick close to the bank. It may look warm, but …

Plenty of opportunity to injure yourself here.

Safety ashore

Unfortunately, the opportunities to damage yourself while camping are numerous. With open fires, hot stoves and activities such as cutting wood and cooking, all undertaken in an unfamiliar environment, the possibilities are almost endless, with injuries that include:

- Cuts
- Burns
- Injuries from falls
- Food poisoning
- Hypothermia
- Insect stings or bites

Tactics to respond to these less than pleasant possibilities are considered in exactly the same way as risks when afloat. They start by looking at methods to reduce the chance of falling foul in the first place, and then ways of dealing with any remaining accidents.

Tactics to avoid problems (precaution)

Avoiding injury in any activity is helped significantly by identifying the risk before starting. In much the same way as the suggested approach while afloat, a moment taken to consider the implications of any new activity can make all the difference. This doesn't just mean general activities, such as pondering whether to attempt to scale a particular crag is a good idea, but, if they are new to you, even the smallest actions. Try to get into the habit of asking yourself such questions as:

- If I jump on this lakeside boulder, will it shift or fall?
- What happens to me if I miss it?
- If I do manage to pull this dead-looking branch down from where it's hung up, where's it going to land?
- Is that cool-looking twig end sticking out of the fire really as finger friendly as it might appear?

In an unfamiliar setting, which your campsite will be, even such questions as – if I step backwards, what's behind me? – can prove helpful.

This sort of low-key but continuous consideration can easily become second nature, and doesn't need to spoil your enjoyment out there. If anything it may well increase it. Nothing ruins a day quite like an injury of course, even a minor one. A simple burn can take the shine off even the best morning.

Whenever about to embark on any activity where there is the potential for injury (and I'm afraid that can be just about anything), it is also worth even the briefest self-reminder that external help will inevitably take some time reaching you, even in the best scenarios.

Woodwork

It almost goes without saying, but particular care needs to be taken when involved with any cutting or chopping of wood. I don't intend to repeat everything already mentioned earlier, but at the same time, the potential for injury in this activity is so great that it felt irresponsible not to mention it again, even if only briefly. So a few thoughts...

I mentioned this when discussing wood splitting, but when felling or trimming branches, dropping down onto one knee can be just as useful a tactic. Where you have to stand, try to angle the stroke to take any misdirected axe head past your body. When stripping branches from a fallen or felled tree, try to keep the trunk between you and the branch you are working on.

Try not to leave axes and saws lying on the ground, and when they aren't in use employ the leather (for the axe) or plastic (for the saw) blade covers.

On a linked theme, if involved in a job that requires intermittent use of a knife, I have to fight the tendency to just put it down between bouts of cutting. I often have to remind myself silently to slip it back into its sheath. The chance of self-mutilation is significantly reduced.

Just consider how far you are from help if things go wrong. Here, at least 20km if I inadvertently fillet a finger.

Keeping the cooking area uncluttered can help to avoid injury.

Two final thoughts regarding all this woodwork: One interesting and not necessarily helpful aspect of wood cutting is that, like cooking, it does tend to attract an audience. This is fine of course, unless they creep in too close. I suspect I need say no more. And the old saying about sharp tools reducing the chance of cutting yourself really is true. Less effort is needed to work a sharp knife, axe or saw. This leaves more muscle power available for control, and less oomph behind the cutting action should things go awry.

Burns

Avoiding burns can be difficult, if not impossible. There are just too many hot things around, in what is inevitably an unaccustomed setting. One way to reduce this risk is to make that setting as familiar as possible. Without even thinking about it these days our tent, and any fire area outside, will tend be laid out in an almost identical way at each site, local conditions allowing. This layout will be too personal to merit illustration, but try to develop your own familiar campsite geography, replicated as much as possible at each location. You will also benefit from scaling this tactic down and applying it your cooking area. This not only helps avoid burns from hot things in unexpected places, but injuries from tripping as well.

Another positive by-product of creating a similar layout at each campsite is that things are so much easier to find when you need them. I suspect that it's not just me that hates losing anything, even relatively briefly. As a naturally untidy person I have to force myself to put the insect repellent back in the correct pocket on the outside of the correct bag for example, before putting that bag where it should always go, just inside the tent entrance on the left. Better than spending ten minutes searching for the bottle as a beautiful sunset fades just beyond the canvas.

One useful move that is less burn prevention and more response, is to have a bowl of cold water close to the fire. If you are prone to minor burns, this can reduce the consequences (see page 208), although by the very nature of canoe camping there is usually a handy river, lake or lump of sea close to hand (there might even be a pun in there somewhere).

Food poisoning

Dire, but very sensible, warnings about not eating anything suspect have already been made. The other form of poisoning that might be encountered by the unfortunate camper comes from the innocent-looking food and drink you brought with you.

All the usual household tactics used to avoid cross contamination around the kitchen are just as valid in the field, just a little harder to put into practice. Two of the biggest problems must be dirty knives and dirty hands.

Much as it might seem a bit overcautious, I am more than happy to use one of those antibacterial gels on my hands after heading for the woods (if you get my drift). It's all too easy to make do with a quick swill in the nearest stream (at least it is for me), but I suspect quite a few cases of gut rot have been avoided by a blob or two of this strange-smelling stuff.

Boiling water.

A citronella candle to repel insects - and the Scottish midge!

I mentioned water way back in the kit section, when I advised carrying a filter. Even where I suspect the water on offer from the nearest stream is perfectly safe I still prefer to see it boiled. True, our recent ancestors often made do without this 'fuss', but then a lot of them ended up collecting something they didn't bargain for when filling a pan at the nearest lake or river. You never know for sure what might be lying in the water just around the next bend. If a fire is going, boiling your drinking water isn't that onerous. The next question is how long should you boil it.

On a topic as important as this, opinions are bound to differ. All I can report is that the advice varies from as soon as a proper rolling boil is achieved (which I suspect will do for all but the rarer tropical nasties) to as much as ten minutes. A number of organisations, including the US Environmental Protection Agency, suggest one minute. For no other reason than it seems a sensible compromise, I tend to go with that.

Filters are easily available, and no trouble to carry. Although probably not quite as effective as boiling, filtering your drinking water, or using one of the recent UV light bug-killing innovations, is certainly the best move when a fire or stove isn't readily available.

Insects

Wee biting beasties. With luck you'll have taken some good, effective insect repellent with you. Whether dealing with Scottish west coast midges (you have now been warned), or Scandinavian mosquitoes (just as bad), coating yourself in something that small flying things consider nasty is sensible.

What that something is depends on the age of the recipient and your attitude towards chemicals. I have what might be a rather overdeveloped mistrust of DEET, particularly when it comes to children (when I have concerns about many of the other constituents in insect repellents too). What I do know is that DEET works. Despite the claims, I suspect that many 'natural' active constituents aren't particularly – active that is. In my experience, based only on unscientific observation, I'd say natural creams and sprays make many flying insects think twice (before biting you anyway), non DEET products put most of them off, while those with DEET in the mix deter all but the most determined. You do have to keep applying them all though, particularly in hot conditions when perspiration can wash it off. If all else fails, consider turning to a head net. Not very pretty, and not much fun to wear, but often better than being eaten alive.

Used as liberally as your fears of chemical poisoning will allow, insect repellent should also help keep ticks at bay (I try to coat my clothing as much as myself – especially socks and trouser bottoms, and specifically when using something containing DEET). Sadly there are a lot of ticks about, particularly where deer are common (therefore all the good bits). I suspect there may be more than ever these days – possibly the result of warmer winters. Lyme disease, sometimes carried by ticks, really can be nasty, particularly if not caught early, and there are even worrying rumours that Tick-borne encephalitis may be about to creep over from the continent. If planning to go to Scandinavia, please look into this grim insect-spread problem (this is one area where, considering the potential consequences of being bitten, I do use DEET).

Boring as it is, particularly in summer, keeping legs covered is a good idea, especially when moving through long grass. And don't just rely on your spray or wipe-on protection. Check yourself each day, and if you have very good friends ask them to share in checking the bits you can't see easily (something to help fill a quiet evening in the tent). Studies suggest that if you remove ticks soon enough, the risk of disease transmission is reduced significantly. Final comment – young ticks can be surprisingly small in spring.

Coping when things do go wrong (response)

I've mentioned first aid kits. The follow up suggestion, if you haven't done it already, is that you find somewhere to learn how to use the contents.

At a rough count I think I've received full first aid training three times, with shorter one-day refreshers or introductory sessions on another four or five occasions. You

It's imortant to know the emergency numbers for the area you're paddling in, and it might not be a bad idea to store them on your phone before setting out.

learn something new each time, and it makes a huge difference to have the confidence in knowing that you are at least able to do something useful should things go wrong. Another avenue is self help, and a good start would be Katherine Wills' book, *Outdoor First Aid*.

For those nasty occasions when you can't manage on your own, the following knowledge is vital:

- Know the emergency service numbers for your locality. For Britain call either 999 or 112. You can then either ask for the Coastguard if you are on the coast, Mountain Rescue if somewhere wild on land, or simply ask for the police if uncertain who it is best to speak to. In Europe 112 is the most universally-used rescue number – although it is also worth identifying the specific numbers used in whatever region you'll be travelling.

- Tucked away in the memory banks the knowledge that the internationally recognised distress signal is six blasts on a whistle or flashes of torch light every minute. To let someone know that you have heard their call for help, and are on your way to provide assistance, three blasts or flashes in the same timeframe is the done thing. I usually have two whistles, one in my rucksack and one in my jacket, both accompanied by a compass.

Although I will repeat my earlier suggestion, and urge anyone going into the wild to find some way of learning about first aid from a qualified instructor, there are a collection of specific problems or injuries, and related responses, that I do intend to discuss here. Based on the latest guidance, some advice must be better than none at all. Just be aware that methods and treatments change quickly. That said, and with a deep breath, these problems or injuries are burns, poisoning and hypothermia.

Treating burns

Given the distinct possibility of using an open fire, and considering that any other form of cooking in the wild will involve situations that even with the best of intents will inevitably fall short of the structured security offered by a kitchen at home, accidents will happen. It's really more a case of when not if.

Minor burns are almost par for the course, with hands most often ending up on the receiving end. These can be treated by placing the offended part in cold water (the colder the better) as quickly as you can find it. If camping in hard winter conditions use snow. Limited blistering may result, but as long as the area affected is small, perhaps no more than 2cm (an inch) across, then everything should look after itself with care and perhaps some painkillers.

The initial tactics are the same with a more serious burn. In this case though, as soon as it is obvious that the damaged area is much bigger, particularly if the skin is badly blistered or broken, then out with the cling film. Either wrap the whole area loosely as best you can (or, as I was advised recently by a paramedic – lay the cling film over the damaged area, and hold in place with loose bandaging), apply more cooling, then transport the poor soul to casualty as soon as possible. Don't move the cling film unless swelling causes it to tighten too much (you'll need to judge this for yourself on the day – and the obvious benefits of the laying on and bandaging method is clear in this case).

If in any doubts about a serious burn, call the emergency services.

This last response also goes for any breakages beyond the odd finger, and any cases of suspected poisoning.

Hypothermia

Anyone spending time outside in Britain or northern Europe runs the risk of hypothermia, especially if spending much time near or on water. Whether when wet outside that brief period we call summer, or exposed to late autumn, winter or early spring conditions, when either not suitably dressed, or incapacitated by injury, fatigue or lack of food and drink – the risk is present.

This isn't just a case of being very cold (although the boundary can be thin), but a state in which the body is unable to maintain its inner heat. The clinical definition of hypothermia is a core temperature below 35°C, but in fact any sustained drop in body warmth can result in this very dangerous condition.

Symptoms of mild hypothermia may be hard to spot, many being the same as those that might be exhibited by anyone who is cold. These include:

· Shivering

· Tiredness

· Lack of energy

· A cold or pale skin

As I said tricky to spot, although lethargy is a good pointer. Possibly the most obvious sign that things are heading the wrong way is your cold friend starting to hyperventilate (breathe fast). As things get a lot more serious, the shivering will become uncontrollable (although this can cease altogether if things get really bad). Other particularly worrying signs include:

· Confusion

· Loss of judgement

· Loss of motor skills (coordination and movement)

· Slurred speech

· Slow or shallow breathing

All these symptoms suggest that hypothermia has set in properly. In extreme cases the victim will become unconscious, with very poor breathing, a weak, irregular or untraceable pulse, and dilated pupils. They may in fact appear dead. Don't give up on them though.

Long before this horrendous point, I hope, you will have called the emergency services. In the tricky position where you can't make contact, and even if you can and are awaiting help, these are the best things you can do for your colleague:

It's surprising how warm it can be inside a bothy bag, even in conditions like these.

- Move them somewhere warm as soon as possible. Not easy I know. A tent is good (preferably with a stove of course). If nothing else, try to get them out of the wind and/or rain/snow. If you have a bothy bag now is the time to use it.

- Wrap them in as much warm stuff as possible – without leaving yourself at risk. Pay particular attention to protecting the head and torso.

- Use your own body heat to help warm them. If things get particularly serious, skin to skin contact is much the most effective way to warm someone. If you have a sleeping bag and/or emergency bag, try to get in there with them. One warning here though – ensure that you don't risk cooling yourself too much. You won't be much help in a hypothermic state yourself.

- Give them warm drinks and high energy food. Hot chocolate drinks would be ideal. One word of caution though – those in a bad way may not be able to swallow, and choking is then a potential risk.

- Once warm – keep them that way for as long as possible.

- Importantly – avoid alcohol. It might sound like a good idea, but a wee dram will only make things worse – trust me.

"Going to the woods is going home."

Final Thoughts

"We shall not cease from exploration

And the end of all our exploring

Will be to arrive where we started

And know the place for the first time."

T.S. Elliot

I touched on the appeal of camping in the introduction. Considering our origins, this attraction is hardly surprising. Having spent all but the last fleeting moments of our development living in small mobile groups, shifting to best advantage through a wild but deeply familiar environment, camping today represents more than a means of mere entertainment or escape from what we have done to our planet. Camping is our heritage, until so very recently our way of life … and we must have been very good at it too. We wouldn't be here in such worryingly large numbers if we hadn't excelled in the skills needed to flourish under those conditions. When you pitch a tent you don't just create a temporary home, you re-enact the normality of our ancestors. As John Muir, the Scottish-born American environmentalist, put it, *"Going to the woods is going home."*

That home comes in two parts, at least before you add the all-important people. First it is the structure you carry with you, the shelter, and then it's the place where you choose to erect that temporary lodging. Both are special. When the best of the two come together, a true wilderness home is created, a fleeting echo of our mobile past. The experience can be almost indescribably uplifting.

Using a canoe, first to carry one crucial element of that home, and then to enable us to reach the other, is to tap into another almost infinitely rich vein of our heritage. Until so very recently there were really only three ways to transport that first element, the tent – on your back, on the back of an animal, or by boat. For the people of the vast boreal forest, endowed with a lot of water, a boat was always likely to be the preferred option, especially when all the raw materials needed to produce it sat conveniently in the woods alongside. The result was the canoe, refined through centuries of use to carry, haul and ultimately to explore.

For me, that is what it is all about, exploration. Whether it is found battling against the flow of a Scandinavian arctic river, flushed with meltwater, trying with aching arms to see what lies around the next pine-fringed corner, or just edging along the shore of an unfamiliar mere in the English Lakes, it is in experiencing the new, the different, that the magic of canoeing lies. Even the keenest of us canoeists spend most of our time viewing the world from the land. Just the sensation of pushing away from an ever more busy shore brings a lift, an instant drug-like hit of freedom, as the firm familiarity of the path or pavement is replaced by the almost-living quiver and rock of the canoe. Each response to tide, wind or current trembles and resonates with uncertainty, mingled with just a hint of possible revelation.

Mankind is meant to move. Being sedentary may suit many of our less savoury ambitions, allowing us to dig and delve, but it appears not to feed the soul. It certainly seems to do little good for our wider home. Once on the move, the appeal of discovery often only grows. To turn back at the end of a day's canoe journey may at first be met only with a feeling of vague dissatisfaction. That feeling, if the turn is repeated, can grow, until one fine day it is just not possible to swing the bow around to point back to where we set out. We have crossed an invisible line.

Then, as old memories return, some perhaps not quite ours alone, we are exploring not just land and waterscapes, we are exploring ourselves. This journey must continue, allowing us to paddle onward, to make landfall far from where we started, somewhere new, somewhere unknown, somewhere exciting, there to make a home, to experience our past, perhaps to consider afresh our future.

Somewhere new, somewhere unknown.

Piteälven, near Arjeplog, northern Sweden

Appendix: List Of Things To Take

This is a list of the kit we usually take canoe camping, arranged in what I hope are convenient groups. In order to keep things simple, additional notes are avoided wherever possible. After all, each item is considered in detail in the What to Take section. Objects marked with an asterisk are probably essential.

Canoe
- Canoe* (with painters at each end)
- Paddles* (one per person, and at least one spare)
- Pfds* (one per person)
- Bailer* (and sponge)
- Loud whistle*
- Cam straps and/or rope* (for tying in a load)
- Throw bag
- Waterproof Curtec pot (or similar) for mobile phone, car/van keys or cameras

Tent
- Tent*
- Groundsheet* (if tent isn't fitted with one)
- Tent pegs*
- A mosquito net (if tent isn't fitted with one)
- A few long tent pegs
- A tarp and/or small tent
- Additional guy rope material
- Candle lamp
- Wind-up torch or lantern

Sleeping
- Heavy-duty dry bag for the following:*
- Sleeping bag* (one per person)
- Dry bag for each sleeping bag*
- Sleeping mat* (closed cell foam or self-inflating, one per person)
- Pillows

Eating kit
- Mug* (one per person)
- Bowl* (at least one per person)
- Cutlery*

Food
Almost impossible to specify, but more than enough for each person for the expected duration of the trip. Probably best to plan for three meals a day, and include snacks. You will burn a lot of calories. Include supplies for hot drinks.
- A food box or Wannigan*
- Cooking oil*
- Salt and pepper
- Stock cubes
- Sugar

Cooking gear

- Heavy-duty bag for cooking gear*
- Gas or liquid fuel stove*
- Matches*
- Dry bag for the matches*
- Wood-fired tent stove (if your tent is designed to take one)
- Fireproof flue arrangement (if using a wood-fired stove)
- Frying pan*
- Saucepan, with lid* (possibly two)
- Heavy iron saucepan with lid
- Kettle (near essential, but you can use a saucepan)
- Kelly Kettle
- Tin foil
- Knife* (dedicated to cooking)
- Spatula or large spoon*
- Chopping board (doesn't need to be big)
- Can opener*
- Washing up liquid* (preferably biodegradable)
- Bottle opener
- Water filter
- Campfire cooking
- Bow saw*
- Knife*
- Tinder*
- Dry bag for tinder*
- Axe (near essential)
- Sharpening stone and/or file for axe and knife (near essential)
- Fire irons
- Wire oven shelf

Repair kit

- Stout bag* (to hold everything)
- Duct tape*
- Plastic pull ties*
- Wire*
- Pliers*
- Araldite* (or similar strong glue)
- String*
- Needle and thread*
- Inflating mat repair kit* (if you have one)

Safety

- Map of the area visited*
- Map case* (if paper maps are used)
- Compass*
- Whistle*
- Knife* (worth repeating)
- Tide timetable* (if on the sea)
- Insect repellent*
- Sun cream*
- Bothy bag (essential if at all cold)
- Length of good rope
- Antibacterial hand wash
- Transistor radio
- Spare batteries for the radio
- Mobile phone

First aid

- Dry bag* (to hold everything)
- Wound dressings*
- Bandages*
- Sticking plasters*
- Micropore*
- Sterile swabs*
- Cling film (perhaps not essential, but a very good idea)

- Antiseptic cream* (such as Savlon)
- Antihistamine cream*
- Antihistamine tablets
- Painkillers* (such as paracetamol)
- Eye wash (again, perhaps not essential, but a very good idea)
- Eye wash bath (ditto)
- Scissors*
- Safety pins*

Clothes
As a minimum per person, in addition to what is already worn.
- Heavy duty dry bag or holdall for the clothes*

Warm weather
- Sun hat*
- Spare shirt*
- Spare trousers*
- Spare underwear*
- Spare socks*
- Thin jumper/fleece*
- Waterproof coat*
- Shorts
- Buff
- Lightweight waterproof trousers
- Sandals (watersport versions possibly best)
- Swimwear

Cold weather (in addition to warm weather clothing)
- Warm hat*
- Warm jumper/fleece*
- Scarf* (or Polar Buff)
- Thick socks*

- Waterproof trousers*
- Gloves*
- Thermal leggings
- Wellies (essential in my books)
- A complete set of spare clothes for each paddler, stored in their own dry bag container*

Severe cold conditions
- Wet suit elements
- Drysuit
- A complete set of spare clothes for each paddler, stored in their own dry bag container*

Personal
- Bag* (shoulder bag or rucksack for everything below)
- Water bottle*
- Headtorch* (or at least some form of torch)
- Spare batteries for the torch*
- Spare compass*
- Spare whistle*
- More matches*
- Dry bag for matches*
- Loo roll*
- Dry bag for loo roll*
- Toiletries (and bag)*
- Insect head net
- Camera
- Sunglasses
- Towel
- Binoculars
- Pencil
- Notebook

The Lofoten islands, northern Norway.

Bibliography

A number of books have been mentioned in this book, and text has been cited from a few more, even an old magazine article. Here is a list of those titles:

Canoeing, Ray Goodwin, Pesda Press 2011, ISBN 9781906095260

Edible Seashore, John Wright, Bloomsbury 2009, ISBN 9780747595311

Explorations in the Great Tuolumne Canon, John Muir, Overland Monthly 1873

Food for Free, Richard Mabey, Collins Gem 2012 (First published 1972), ISBN 9780007183036

Outdoor First Aid: A Practical Manual, Katherine Wills, Pesda Press 2103, ISBN 9781906095352

Path of the Paddle, Bill Mason, (out of print but you may be able to find it second hand)

Survival in Cold Water, C. Brooks, Survival Systems Ltd. 2001

The Singing Wilderness, Sigurd Olson University of Minnesota Press 1997 (first published 1956), ISBN 9780816629923

Ultimate Navigation Manual, Lyle Brotherton, Harper Collins 2011, ISBN 9780007424603

Wild Food, Ray Mears and Gordon Hillman, BBC 2007, ISBN 9780340827901

Woodcraft and Camping, George Sears (Nessmuk), Dover Publications Inc. 2003 (First published 1920), ISBN 9780486211459

Index